Ian On The  *le*

of Sheffield and the Peak District

Ian D. Rotherham

2008

I'd like to dedicate this little book to the memories of five local environmental champions, good friends and greatly missed: Les Harris, Oliver Gilbert, Pete Bowler, Sheilagh Howe, and Tony Turner. The world is a lesser place without them.

Published by:
Wildtrack Publishing
Venture House
105 Arundel Street
Sheffield
S1 2NT
UK

ISBN 978-1-904098-13-3

Cover photograph © Ian Rotherham

Printed by B & B Press Ltd., Parkgate, Rotherham

Frontispiece: The Wild Fig now naturalised along the Rivers Don, Sheaf and Porter, and though an alien species, it is specially protected here as a culturally important plant symbolic of Sheffield's industrial past. © Ian Rotherham

Acknowledgements

I wish to acknowledge all those who have taken part in the BBC programmes or have read and written in to *The Star* newspaper column. I'm especially grateful to those whom have sent in pictures and anecdotes many of which are featured here. I would also like to thank Paul Hobson for the use of some of his excellent photographs of birds and mammals. If you want to see more or to commission his work then go to his web site; http://www.paulhobson.co.uk – prepare to be impressed!

I'd also like to thank, very belatedly, my parents, for their reluctant faith that there might after all be a job in natural history and wildlife. If they were alive today then they would be reassured that not becoming a Doctor of Medicine wasn't such a bad decision after all. I'm also very grateful to my former Deputy Headmaster at King Edward VII School in Sheffield, Mr Arthur Jackson, who, when sharing my parents' concerns over my career choice, found the then new and indeed unique degree course in Ecology at Lancaster University.

Thanks also to many friends such as Paul Ardron with whom I've shared a lifelong enthusiasm and many cold, wet field trips, and Christine Handley for interest and support, and many others, too numerous to mention, along the way. There's an especially big thanks to my wife Liz for putting up with all of this.

Longshaw Sunset. © Ian Rotherham

A SHORT PREAMBLE

From Martin Smith of *The Sheffield Star* in conversation with environmentalist and champion for nature, Ian Rotherham

The beginning

From the house where Ian Rotherham grew up he could hear the boom of the steelworks' forges and see the Don Valley sky lit up by their mighty blast furnaces. He would walk to Norton County School up Warminster Road with a scarf across his face to keep out the smoke and stink; then he would see the yellow gunge it filtered out and swore he would try to change the world. And he did. Later, as a teenager, he would walk down the steep slope through the haven of Meersbrook Park and experience the massed flocks of summer Swifts, skimming at head height, but with the degraded and polluted vision of the City of Sheffield sprawling out across the wide flood plains of the Rivers Sheaf and Don ahead of him. The clinging smog and polluted rivers that blighted Sheffield's green spaces and threatened its two million trees drove Ian to become a world-renowned environmentalist and champion for nature. So Ian Rotherham PhD, ecology expert, university lecturer and Sheffield United fanatic, has spent much of his working life trying to undo the damage done by centuries of heavy industry. Now he wants the new and emerging Sheffield to take its environmental responsibilities seriously; before it's too late.

'*I grew up in Sheffield at the end of its great industrial era*' said former King Edward VII Grammar School boy Ian. '*You can see the whole of the city from where we used to live in Meersbrook. There was an amazing variety of smells coming from the factories as I walked down the hill and over Sheaf Bridge to catch the bus - vinegar from the 'pickling' of metal at Tyzack's, mint and sugar from Dixon's mint factory - it was a peculiar combination. Even as* small kids we were aware of pollution and knew that a river full of sewage was probably a bad thing.'

'As a kid I hated all that Don Valley industrial area. It was three miles of Dante's inferno from the city centre to the M1.' But the smog and muck fired a passion for wildlife that still motivates Ian today. 'We would spend weekends in Rivelin or Moss Valley' said 50-year-old Ian, who now lives in Norton and is Reader responsible for Sheffield Hallam University's Tourism and Environmental Change Research Unit. 'I grew up with a passion for the outdoors, birds, insects and plants. I have wanted to change the world since I was 10 years old and make a difference but it's the economists and politicians that actually do things. We have to find a way of getting them to see the environment is central to everything we do. To make them realise the environment and tourism can be the big earners for a place like Sheffield.'

'Sheffield people have always been at the centre of things with a passion for the countryside. They were involved in the protest for freedom to roam on the moors and the Peak National Park was created because people demanded it. Places like Norfolk Park, the Loxley Valley and Shire Brook Valley have seen some great work but we aren't always very good at keeping them up; the funding is always under pressure and the best staff often move on quickly to other jobs. The environment is considered a luxury but it isn't. It has to be central to plans. It is the most important thing to everyone. We have to make it a priority.'

Weasel. © Steve Smith

When he's not fighting the forces of environmental evil, bird watching or working in his garden, Ian follows one of his other great loves - Sheffield United.

'From our front garden you could hear the roar of the crowd from Bramall Lane and you could tell which team had scored because of the different sound of the celebrations' said Ian, who invested in a season ticket for United's season back in the Premiership, and is looking forward to their return. 'Everybody used to walk to the games and the streets were thronged with people on match days. When I was young they were getting 40,000 crowds. It sounds like old man's memories but that's what it was like. I looked forward to the Premiership season with some trepidation having hoped for a big signing or two before the start, but it didn't happen. I'd hoped we'd get a 'take-no-prisoners' midfielder with a bit of skill who could score goals, a new Michael Brown, but we didn't. Then with the West Ham debacle, the rest as they say is history. But there's always the next time.'

Common Toad. © Ian Rotherham

Some might describe Ian as a take-no-prisoners environmentalist, but no-one could accuse him of not living in the real world. 'The City Council's website for example, shows us projects around the city and says people are involved but the majority aren't', said the former head of the Sheffield City Council's Ecological Advisory Service. 'There's a lot of hype about various initiatives, but a lot of it, in the words of Humphrey Bogart, doesn't add up to a hill of beans. We could help the Health Service and lessen the burden on other services by giving people a higher quality environment to live in. It is proved that a good environment means people are physically and mentally healthier. What we *need is a quality green space on every doorstep, and ways to stop organisations like Bradfield Parish Council ploughing it up on a whim. The people we have to influence are the movers and shakers, the politicians and planners, and find a way that they can buy into the ideas. There are all sorts of initiatives about people's lifestyles and a healthy life but when it comes down to it, what wins out every time is short-term economic gain.'*

'What I am passionate about is letting Sheffield people have an everyday contact with nature. Almost everyone you talk to loves wildlife, from the most senior politicians to little kids and grandparents. People like nature and see the benefits of a healthy and diverse environment but when it comes down to making economic and planning decisions they behave selfishly. The point they miss is that it makes good economic sense to look after the environment. The government is always going on about joined-up thinking and that's what we need. A problem is that the investment and the cash benefits go to different people and Government finds support difficult to justify. Investment in say countryside management doesn't necessarily bring financial rewards for the Government department in question. However, it does make money for other people, such as local business, and it saves the Treasury huge amounts on the health bills, etc., and so you are talking different budget heads and paper walls and silos. However, work we've been doing at Hallam University does confirm that investment in say National Parks services or in countryside management does reap rewards through tax revenue to Government too. The problem here is that we are not good at accounting for this sort of thing, and for the environmental professionals this is the boring stuff. Visitors go to an area and they spend cash in that area, and both business and the Government make money. It's simple. Take the RSPB in the Dearne Valley as an example. The project has turned around people's perceptions of the area, it has helped rejuvenate the local economy, and so create business opportunities. The RSPB employ staff there and they spend money in the local economy too. Believe it or not, the RSPB Dearne Valley project will generate a tourism

visitor economy of around 100,000 visitors a year, and that is worth at least 1.5 million pounds a year; and it's sustainable. There is even more dramatic value if you look at local people's health and well-being and also what we call the provision of ecological services like flood prevention by the site; that amounts to 100s of millions of pounds. But to get that benefit you need to invest in infrastructure and in people. You need to spend money to make money and we don't like paying taxes to do that!'

'People often see the big picture but don't identify with their own individual actions. It is all the actions that stack up to the global crisis we have now. I want to help individuals to take action to change things; and it must change quickly to avoid catastrophe.'

So, alien species, climate change and a diminished planetary eco-system; is this Dr Who or Star Trek? No, this is Sheffield, South Yorkshire, and every other place on earth. Ian Rotherham is not a merchant of doom on any of these issues but he does see problems ahead. *'Things are going to have to change because of the environment, things are happening incredibly quickly'*, he said. *'People are frightened about global instability and they are questioning the way we do things. The way we have changed the planet's eco-system over the last 500 years has been huge. It's not just about creating carbon dioxide that is causing climate change. We have changed the landscape of the planet with industrialisation and urbanisation. Look at the amount of energy we use and the heat we create. We have changed the way the planet responds and a lot of what we are seeing is because of that.'*

The wild Rhododendron. © Ian Rotherham

On the issue of alien species, Ian is an expert on the aggressive *Rhododendron* plant - reintroduced to Britain in 1763, after disappearing from these islands during the last Ice Age. '*For a lot of people alien species or plants brought to this country from abroad are a huge issue. There is a risk of the 'Disneyfication' of the plant world where everywhere has the same species; the Big Mac of ecology. At first it feels like diversity because there are more varieties, but often the incomers drive out the native species and eventually there is less variety. It is a huge issue around the world. But many plants are established here now and give tremendous pleasure; so it's a difficult balance. In many cases we need to learn to live with the aliens and try to minimise the adverse effects. I suspect that most environmentalists still don't understand this.*'

The environment affects us all and must be at the heart of our future planning

A small shift in thinking could transform Sheffield's environment. Ecology expert Ian Rotherham believes it's time to put environmental issues at the top of the planning agenda, with cash up front. '*I'm not against*

development but the environment has to be at the centre of our thinking, not an afterthought,' said Ian, now Reader at Sheffield Hallam University's Tourism and Environmental Change Research Unit. '*If one per cent of the cost of every building development went towards paying for environmental projects, it would transform the face of this city and every other city. If Sheffield wants to be a world leader in parks access, access to green spaces and the Peak District, we need to be more imaginative. We are still governed by short-term thinking. If every development had to have an environmental audit to make sure it was at least environmentally neutral, things would improve tremendously. A good environment makes sound economic sense and people would enjoy the improvements. The Shire Brook Valley was running with raw sewage in the 1980s. It was terrible. But now, after being managed by successive projects, the area is a nature reserve. The Don and Rother were two of the dirtiest rivers in Europe, but are now clean again. There is, of course, still a toxic legacy in the sediments of the river beds and floodplains, but nobody really wants to discuss that, let alone do anything about it. People said these things couldn't be done but they have been. That type of transformation can happen elsewhere if resources are put in. The environment means something to everybody but when it comes to decision making it's treated as peripheral. It's not; it's essential. But also it's not free.*'

This is the aptly named *Phallus impudicus* or Stinkhorn Fungus. These emerge from a white gelatinous egg to produce the most awful stink which attracts flies that disperse the spores. You can have great fun by placing one in a polythene bag in a strategic location, as we did when I was a postgraduate student at Sheffield University, in my boss's office. The *Phallus* emerges over a couple of days and proves that the molecules are sufficiently small to get through the minute pores in the polythene. Happy days!

SOME TIPS FOR GOING WILD

1. JOIN the Wildlife Trust or the RSPB. Get involved locally and take responsibility for your own patch.

2. GET others involved - especially children. Take the kids for a day out to the RSPB Dearne Valley Nature Reserve.

3. RECORD wildlife in your area in pictures. Start a website and look at the Natural History Society website.

4. WRITE to or email your MP and tell him or her that you are concerned about the environment in your area. Ask what they are doing about it on your behalf.

5. SEND emails and letters to *The Star* with questions, and let us know what you are doing for wildlife and the environment.

A full moon over White Edge lodge and the Grouse Inn at Froggatt. © Ian Rotherham

BY WAY OF INTRODUCTION

The media and communication

I've always worked closely with the local media, on both environmental issues and more generally talking about, and hopefully enthusing about, wildlife and nature. *The Sheffield Star* and *BBC Radio Sheffield* have always been interested and supportive about such matters, and so it seemed a natural partnership to team up on this. I'd worked with Paul Licence, Martin Smith and Steve Caddy on *The Star* in setting up and promoting the *Sheffield Wildlife Action Partnership* to establish nature reserves and educational projects across the region, and we raised around £1 million pounds over ten years to do this. When *The Star* approached me about writing the *On the Wild Side* column it seemed a good idea and the right thing to do. Rony Robinson had long been a contact and friend at Radio Sheffield, though over the years I've worked with many different reporters and presenters. A bit like *The Star*, when *Radio Sheffield* suggested that we do a regular phone-in it was a great opportunity to link to the newspaper column. From a personal point of view it is chance to talk to and even meet loads of people across the region, and I hope though this to both support what they do and to pass on my enthusiasm and passion for the subject. That's my aspiration and I think sometimes we achieve it. I also always find the local and regional media are able to give issues much more considered thought and time than the national ones. The latter are generally looking for a slick headline and a sharp sound-bite – their audiences demand it!

Sheffield and the Peak

I grew up in part in the middle of Sheffield, around Heeley, Meersbrook and Norton, and in part out in the Peak District moorlands. My first experiences of the Peak were days out at Longshaw as a very small child, and then later to the magnificent Burbage Valley. However, probably the most significant thing was that my Aunt Di and Uncle Gilbert had a bungalow at Lodge Moor, and from there was the gateway to Rivelin and its heaths and Dams, to Wyming Brook, and thence to Redmires and Stanage. I still think that we don't fully appreciate what a fortunate location we in Sheffield have when it comes to the natural environment. This was also a time when children even as young as four or five years of age were allowed to roam for several hours away from home and for distances of three or four miles or so. Of course, there were no computer games then so we had to make our own entertainment. The other areas to which we went as small children included the Gleadless Valley as it was being bulldozed into form as a suburb of Sheffield from its ancient origins as a Derbyshire rural landscape. Its name rather evocatively means '*The clearing of the Red Kite*'. Further afield was the still rural, and largely still Derbyshire, Moss Valley running east-west just south of Sheffield. Here, there was the gauntlet to run of gamekeepers and irate farmers who really didn't want us town kids running amok in their valley. Thus began a long-term game of '*hide-and-seek*'; mostly with us hiding and them seeking. A slightly more legitimate playground was the extensive green spaces afforded by Graves Park, courtesy of Alderman Graves and his visionary bequests to the people and City of Sheffield. Here, there were still the dreaded park-keepers or '*parkies*', but they were pretty tame compared with the gamekeepers. Our favourite places to go were the more remote and overgrown woodlands where you could make dens and also, and importantly, dams. I was brought up on a diet of books about both wildlife, which by about five years of age, was already an obsession, and Enid Blyton's *Secret Seven*, and Arthur Ransome's

Swallows and Amazons. A key feature of the latter was the concept of kids being able to boat freely across either Lake Windermere or the Norfolk Broads or anywhere else for that matter. There was the Boating Lake at Graves Park but you had to pay, the time was limited, and the whole experience was closely supervised by the aforementioned parkies. It seemed that you needed two basic things to act out *Swallows and Amazons*, and both were in desperately short supply if you grew up in Meersbrook. One of these was a boat, though that could be solved by a tin bath or other similar makeshift floating object. The other more difficult requirement was for a large water-body onto which this '*boat*' might be launched. This is where the idea of building a dam came in. It seemed to us as bright young minds that the problem could be solved by damming the stream in either or both Graves Park (the Graves Park Beck), or in what we called Cat Lane Woods (Ashes Wood in the Gleadless Valley). I think the idea was that somehow the water would back up sufficiently to allow a large enough body of water for us to attempt to float our boat, or at least a home-made raft. Sadly this never came to be, at least not to its fullest extent; though we were assured by one of the parkies who caught us, that when our last dam had finally burst we had caused a major flood incident affecting houses at Woodseats. So not such a bad dam then!

Sheffield from Derbyshire Lane close to where I grew up; painted by the famous artist Turner but a little before my time. © Sheffield Galleries

I'm told by my former school friend Peter Gribbon, who is now a '*little mester*' at Abbeydale Hamlet, that we used to climb up onto the roof of the parky's little house overlooking the Graves Park Boating Lake and place turves of grass over his chimney. He was there all snug and cosy with a little coal-fired stove, and the intention was apparently to '*smoke him out*'; though of course I deny this totally and absolutely. Needless to say the parky in question was not pleased by our efforts.

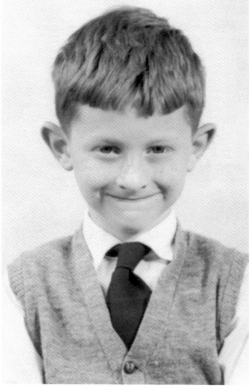

The young naturalist

I think access to countryside, albeit sadly impoverished in terms of many of the plants and animals that should have been there if pollution and persecution hadn't taken their tolls, was hugely important to me. By the age of four I was already hooked on natural history and wildlife and by not a lot older than that local neighbours and others would bring me specimens they had found for me to identify or comment on. One of my close friends at the time was Ian Osborn and we would take all sorts of natural history items for the class '*nature table*'. Our speciality in the autumn was to arrive with handfuls of the large Garden Spider, the one which makes the gorgeous orb-webs. These were collected from hedgerows *en route* either to or from school. Those along the old gennel off Warminster Road I recollect as being the best. Mum was not well

pleased when I arrived home clutching about ten large spiders and struggling to keep them all in my grasp.

When television arrived I was enthralled by Peter Scott and his wildlife programmes on the BBC. This opened up a whole world which I had never realised existed. In my teens I did meet him at Slimbridge Wildfowl Centre but was too dumbstruck to say anything at all meaningful. I still regret that. But for childhood heroes, a combination of Sir Peter Scott, believe it or not Charles Darwin (after someone gave me a book on evolution and the diversity of life), Tony Currie who wore number 10 for Sheffield United, Geoffrey Boycott who batted for Yorkshire, and Justin Haywood (the lead singer of the Moody Blues), must count as a fairly eclectic mix. But of all these it was the first two that caught my imagination and passion for the natural world. This, however, was tempered by the sometimes grim reality of growing up in a dirty and polluted city from which beautiful nature seemed to have been heartlessly and ruthlessly driven. Even from this very early age it seemed wrong and almost inhuman that humanity should do this to itself and to nature. Yet there were few signs of anyone willing or able to do much about it. The RSPB was not the huge and dynamic body it is today, and the Wildlife Trusts were mostly just a twinkle in the eye. Other organisations like Friends of the Earth and Greenpeace were only just beginning to emerge.

Longshaw as evening falls. © Ian Rotherham

No more heroes

I've always felt that it was important to get people involved and re-connected to nature. I grew up in the latter days of the industrialisation of our region and witnessed some of the worst aspects of environmental degradation and social exclusion. Even as a child I felt that somehow it wasn't right, and 'someone' should do something about it. I suppose too, that I grew up on a diet of TV heroes when we only had two TV channels and my favourite as a young child was *Robin Hood*, three times a week, starring Richard Green. In fact I think the only prize I won at Infant School was for a fancy dress competition and I swept the opposition aside not only with my wonderful green and red Robin Hood outfit, but also a song. The older readers will recall the theme tune to the TV Robin Hood; well that was my winning ploy. I can't remember what the prize was, but Robin Hood carried the day. All the old Westerns had a hero, or for the cavalry to ride in and save the day, but observing the raw sewage in the River Sheaf in the 1960s and 1970s it seemed that environmental heroes were decidedly thin on the ground. The heavy pall of smoke which hung over much of the city in the 1950s and early 1960s didn't help my mood or my health. Looking back as a young child I always had bronchitis and tonsillitis, and so did most of my friends. It is sometimes hard to believe how Sheffield has changed since then; by the 1960s and 1970s we were justifiably proud of being the '*Clean Air City*'. It is such a dramatic change that it is almost inconceivable that people lived and worked in such appalling conditions. The truth is that after all the hardships of previous centuries people were just glad to have a job, a place to live and food to eat. A nice or even healthy environment was often considered a luxury. When people talk of going back to '*Victorian values*' it is worth considering cholera and typhoid, child abuse, stinking rivers, smogs and a bit of starvation, but I suppose you can't have everything. By the 1960s, of course, we had also acquired DDT, much welcomed by troops in the Second World War to get rid of ticks, mites and fleas. I remember my dad telling me how they all got dusted down with DDT powder and were pleased to be rid of the pests and parasites. By the 1960s, we were also rid of every bird of prey apart from Kestrels, and also lost all the fish-eating species like Heron, Great Crested Grebe and Kingfisher. Yet the advance of technology and science had also brought huge benefits, it just seemed a shame that we couldn't

apply the discoveries and inventions in a way that didn't hurt people and the environment. I guess we are still struggling with this one.

Something else that the Victorians gave us was the common invasive plants like Himalayan Balsam and Japanese Knotweed. These have become a big part of my research interest after I did a PhD at Sheffield University studying invasion by *Rhododendron ponticum*. When, as a teenager and keen bird-watcher, we used to go to *Rhododendron* sites in search of roosting birds, say at Cordwell, or breeding Nightingales at Clumber Park, I had no idea that it wasn't native. We also gained Buddleia during the late 1800s, and unlike *Rhododendron* which most conservationists hate, we all love '*The Butterfly Bush*'.

A Badger road casualty. © Ian Rotherham

By the 1970s, we'd also lost almost all our Badger population, and mostly through illegal Badger digging. It seems ironic now that despite scientific evidence that it won't solve problems of Bovine TB in cattle, there are endless calls from some sections of Government and agencies, and across a lot of the farming sector, for moves to cull and eradicate Badgers. There must be better ways to resolve this, such as mass inoculation and perhaps some basic hygiene management by the farming industry. To the majority of the British public, to go back to legalised Badger persecution would be just unacceptable, and bear in mind that we would be paying for the pleasure too. There is a serious problem for cattle farming but this cannot be the answer. At a time when the farming industry is trying to reinvent itself and also gain a new awareness by the public though local foods and farm tourism, *etc.*, this would be a huge PR disaster. Local MP Peter Hardy pioneered the early Badger protection laws and helped steer them through Parliament. His actions support one of my core premises on the environment, which is that it is individuals who can and must make a difference. You can have all the policies and bureaucracy in the world, but it is individual champions that make change happen. Peter's legacy is one that we must now be vigilant to protect.

Across our region it is local people who have driven through projects and support for things like access to the countryside, freeing up the moorlands that were for so long locked away from the common people. They have promoted and funded environmental education centres and projects, and they have campaigned to safeguard our unique natural areas. It is local champions who battled to save moorlands and other areas from paper pulp tipping, and worse, but with little or no support from the powers that be, until the very end. The damage to lands, particularly around Bradfield, throughout the 1980s and 1990s must count as one of the worst ever concerted acts of environmental vandalism in or around a National Park. Ultimately the firm responsible for generating the paper pulp waste was owned by an American parent company. This is ironic really when you think how strictly the National Parks are protected in the USA, that they can operate over here in such a cavalier way. There will always remain the questions raised by the late Les Harris and by David Barker, over what was underneath the paper pulp as well. We will never know for sure. Many campaigns like that to halt the paper pulp tipping had limited success; we lost a huge amount of landscape and wildlife habitat. But we can be sure that without the massive efforts of a few campaigners, much more would have gone. It takes local people to stand up and be counted and not to be frightened by the bully-boy tactics. It is our environment and we have a duty and a responsibility to care for it and hand it on intact to future generations. Too often we fail miserably to do even the most basic things to maintain the natural resource. But think about the victories and the things which we now take for granted. Everyone who walks over the moors around Fox House, Longshaw and Blacka Moor, or out along the Mayfield Valley, owes a debt of gratitude to Gerald Haythornthwaite and the

others in the CPRE who battled to stop Sheffield expanding and sprawling out westwards; the body odour of urban development. Without their vision and efforts and the cash from Alderman Graves, none of that would be there today.

A Common Lizard on my arm. This is on the moors saved by Alderman Graves. © Ian Rotherham

This was down to individuals with commitment and vision; not enlightened planning. We must never take all these good things for granted. Even the National Parks have only been around since the 1950s, and our Country Parks are even more recent. Yet, like the absence of visual air pollution, it is too easy to assume it has always been so. The reality is that it is only so today, because a handful of people cared enough to do something about it, turning concern and aspiration into action.

A lonesome Pine? © Ian Rotherham

Accepting the unacceptable

It always surprises me how so many people simply accept the unacceptable in their own environment. Maybe we've somehow been worn down over the decades and the centuries to be too passive. There's also the assumption of course that '*someone else will deal with it*', that '*they probably know best*', and indeed '*that there is no alternative*'. On all counts this is usually wrong. When I worked as Sheffield City Council's Ecologist I would guess that around 50% of problem cases were easily avoidable when discussed between '*stakeholders*', another 30-40% could be resolved reasonably easily and any damage mitigated or compensated for. That leaves around 10-20% which were serious problems and required significant intervention to resolve. In a very few cases there was no way round a conflict and if the proposal went ahead the interest and value of a site was lost or irreparably damaged. In some cases there might be an over-riding reason why a development should then go ahead, but if that is the case then there really should be significant compensation through provision of a new high-quality site elsewhere. This rarely happened or happens today. Furthermore, if the site under threat was of major wildlife or heritage value then there should be no question of its loss being allowed. We were always encouraged to find ways to compromise, and with robust policy and planning guidance turned into enlightened action that could reap rewards for the environment and for local people. Yet so often opportunities are spurned and compromise means long-term decline and loss. I recall back in the 1980s, then veteran access and environmental campaigner and rambler, Stephen Morton, giving his forcibly held view that '*…compromise was defeat by instalments*'. I fear that he was right.

One of the region's losses: the Red Squirrel. In the 1980s, not a single one of the region's conservation agencies would help a campaign to save them – until they had already gone. © Paul Hobson

One of the major difficulties we seem to face is that we only protect what the experts consider to be the best and the irreplaceable. When we drew up the '*Sheffield Nature Conservation Strategy*' in 1991, the survey and audit of our environmental resources suggested that in the entire region we had only two plant species that were recognised as of national significance and therefore worthy of protection. One of these was certainly introduced and the other was of '*doubtful origin*'. Of course this was total rubbish in terms of assessing how important the local environmental resource, which included a big chunk of the Peak District National Park, really was. But this was based on the guidance and methodologies that were used at the time, and they failed to recognised issues of local quality and of local distinctiveness. Even now we still hide behind the words of policies and strategies that promise a lot but protect and deliver very little. A few years ago there was a big announcement that areas of land which had been '*unimproved*' (i.e. not been ploughed up or had fertiliser or other chemical additives applied) for a given number of years would be henceforth protected. This, we were told by senior officers of Government agencies, would protect landscape archaeology and heritage, and all the now rare animals and plants associated with old meadows and pastures. Yet the implementation of what was an EU driven directive is full of Weasel-words. The process is limited and naive and the environmental agencies do not have the staff to apply the law to protect our heritage. So sites under 2 hectares are mysteriously exempted; not a legal exemption that we can debate and discuss democratically, but a bureaucratic tool to make workloads easier. I discussed this with a senior officer at Defra, the Governments main parent body for environmental matters, and they backed off from applying the guidance, even on large sites which merited protection, because a fat-cat judge had made a punitive ruling against Defra in favour of a landowner. This basically challenged the definition of '*unimproved*' to rule that if land '*was capable of being so improved*' and the farmland around had been '*improved*', then converting an ancient meadow to arable or to '*improved*' grassland should not be deemed '*improvement under the Act*'. Defra was fined a lot of money and was henceforth running scared; too scared to protect our landscape with laws that already existed. Of course none of this was publicly stated. I think we can rest assured where the fat cat judge's allegiances lay, and also that in all probability he didn't look out from his living room over a degraded and knackered landscape. Maybe I'm guilty of making assumptions about his style and place of residence but I suspect not.

Common Soft Rush in the snow at Curbar. © Ian Rotherham

Quality, quality, quality

I should emphasise that in terms of environmental quality, when we talk about '*improved*' and '*unimproved*' lands these are agricultural or farming terms. As a rough guidance this relates to the process which from the 1940s to the 1990s destroyed 98% of the region's hay meadows and pastures, and many heathland areas too. '*Unimproved*' sites are fantastic for wildlife, teeming with insects such as butterflies, and many wildflowers, and so rich for mammals and birds too. They gave the rural and the urban-fringe landscapes much of their unique qualities in terms of colour, texture, sound and even fragrance; and they've mostly gone. '*Improved*' generally means productive with added fertiliser and major carbon-debt, and very green (in colour at least), but of almost zero value to wildlife, archaeology or heritage = knackered and degraded. In the period from 1940 to 1990, even the Peak National Park lost 95% of these rich and irreplaceable landscapes. To add insult to injury, most if not all of this loss was avoidable and was not the fault of individual farmers. We the public paid for the process through taxes and hence subsidies; and we the public drive it through a demand for cheap food and a corporate ignorance of the processes and impacts of food production. The issues are clouded by the Weasel-words and the double-speak through which people were educated or miseducated about the environment and farming over the same period. Over this time there was a desperate drive to produce food in the post-War '*island-under-siege*' mentality, but at a huge cost in terms of petrochemically and financially

Questions I've been asked

Why do moths fly towards lights? Well, it is because they navigate by the moon and they think the light or candle is it. This means that they fly in ever decreasing circles towards the light and ultimately crash land into it. And no they don't deliberately fly into people or attempt to get tangled in your hair. They are just disorientated

LOCAL ACTION – it is down to *you*!!

Unfortunately a lot of local people think there is someone taking care of your environment on your behalf. There isn't, so it is up to you to be vigilant and to do what you can.

subsidised processes. Old and traditional were deemed bad and outmoded, and new and techno-fix processes were good. The aims were high input and output farming and fewer people involved and employed. Food production became an industry and the outputs were processed and packaged beyond the pale of the rest of our increasingly urban society. So within only a few decades the landscape has been largely degraded, and in many ways worse still, food and food production have been separated from, and are mostly outside the experience of, most people. The public are then reduced simply to '*consumers*', increasingly ignorant of the economically-functioning countryside and the farming industry; the latter has become agri-industry and itself often separated from the living land which spawned it. Now, belatedly, politicians and economic planners talk of sustainable farming, of quality of life, and of '*green infrastructure*'. We have '*Biodiversity Action Plan Targets*' and aim for '*low carbon lifestyles*'. In my humble opinion, a bit bloody late!

Nightjar is a bird of heath and common. © Paul Hobson

I'm an ecologist and a landscape historian and I just can't help thinking that the problems really began with the famous or infamous '*parliamentary enclosures*'. This was the process in the 1700s and 1800s, when the landscape was largely wrested from the common people and vested in the fat cats of agricultural big business. Perhaps this is where the separation began, when the commons were stolen from the commoners. The reality is clearly far too complex to discuss here, but I can't help thinking this is where it all began to go pear-shaped. There's some great educational

work being done now to try and re-build these connections, but it seems to have taken the total destruction of the ecological and much of the heritage resource, the whole pesticide and pollution crisis of the 1960s-1990s, plus a dash of BSE, Foot-and-Mouth Disease, a collapse in the farming economy, and now massive floods and catastrophic droughts to make planners and other decision-makers question what has been going on. How can we be so blind for so long? I suspect that a part of the problem is the age-old dilemma between long-term and short-term benefits and necessities, and also the conflict between personal gain and public good. With environmental quality and quality of life it seems that we have been dominated by short-term incentives and personal vested interests for far too long. The public good and the long-term benefit have dropped off the corporate radar of a consumer-driven and a corporately irresponsible and unresponsive society. Surely our children have a '*right*' to walk through fields of Ox-eye Daisies, and ancient woods full of Bluebells. It must be morally and ethically wrong to take that away from them. I recall back in the 1980s, at the zenith of agricultural intensification and the loss of almost all farm and other ponds in the region, there was a real chance that in many parts of the country, the Common Frog would become extinct. Imagine having to explain to the kids what a Frog was because they had never seen one. The Frog was largely rescued by an upsurge in locally-based actions generated by environmentalists such as Sheffield's own BBC wildlife gardener Chris Baines. Huge numbers of people went out and dug new village ponds, school wildlife garden ponds, and back garden ponds. The individual actions made a massive difference. You might say that such an extinction, and occurring so rapidly, could never happen. My reply is that here in the heart of Sheffield in the 1930s and 1940s, the local children would often have seen Red Squirrels in their gardens, Harvest Mice in the farmland, and would have still heard Corncrakes in Gleadless and on the Manor. Within ten to twenty years all these had gone, and with DDT pesticide pollution, the Sparrowhawks, Peregrines, Great Crested Grebes, Herons, and Kingfishers, were all close behind. So beware of complacency and of the assumptions that it could never happen.

Ancient habitat for wild flowers, Water Voles and Butterflies: Kaye Meadows destroyed in 2008 by Bradfield Parish Council. © Ian Rotherham

Decline, fall and denial

In my experience almost none of the environmental disasters which have occurred have done so because an individual or even a corporate body decided to go out and deliberately trash the wildlife or its habitat. No, it is always that '*they aren't having any real impact and so it is not significant*', and their important needs are so vital that a few Ox-eye Daisies and Bluebells shouldn't stop progress should they? The last one from Bradfield Parish Council when they brutally rotovated the '*Site of Scientific Interest*' wildflower and Water Vole site at Kaye Meadows in 2008, was that they were doing this to improve local biodiversity! Wow, that is double-speak worthy of George Orwell. It is the basic denial of the facts and the need to take responsibility for the consequences of your actions that lie at the core of what I am saying. With Kaye Meadows, not only did the Parish Council not go through any worthwhile process of impact assessment and mitigation, but they went ahead despite huge local protest, and in the month of August. Now here the story gets worse, because for a tall herb wet meadow this is just when all the baby froglets and young toads are out and about, having left their breeding sites. So in that case, even if it was decided to plough up a site like this, then for heaven's sake don't do it at that time of year. If the meadow is about 100m x 100m that is 10,000 square metres; and if we assume there is just one baby Frog and one baby Toad in each square metre, then Bradfield Parish Council just authorised the rotovating of 10,000 baby Frogs

and 10,000 baby Toads. Did they put up they hands and pass a motion to do this in their council meeting? I don't think they did; but that is what they achieved on behalf of their parishioners and it is not a record to be proud of. Explain that to the kids when they ask '*what does sustainability mean*' and '*what do grown-ups mean by quality of life*'. Amphibians sometimes get accidentally killed by lawn-mowers in long wet grass and if you've ever done that you'll know it isn't pretty. Well imagine 20,000 times that and all deliberate and unnecessary. Not nice!

Burnet Moth on Knapweed Flower before the rotovator struck. © Ian Rotherham

Part of my problem with all this is the fact that it is unnecessary and could easily have been avoided. In the Kaye Meadows case there should have been a standard process of assessment and then a proper local consultation. This was not done and the Parish Council clearly showed scant regard for conservation policy and also for its statutory duty to pay due heed to matters of biodiversity conservation. No, it is the disregard for local people and also the fact that in society today we can't wait a little while to get it right – we want stuff at all cost and we want it now. In this case Sheffield City Council had committed to work with what is England's second largest parish, to find an alternative and more suitable location. But no, we must have it now and damn the consequences. Worse still, those behind such demands are so dishonest about what the impacts will be. I'd have more respect for them if they at least said yes it will cause damage but we really don't care. To claim that somehow this is going to be '*good for the environment*' and '*good for wildlife*', is really too much. Let's at least have a little more honesty and less denial. We want what we want and we don't give a damn would at least be a little more open and honest.

Stealing the environment from the next generation

A central part of the concept of the idea of sustainable development is that each generation should live within its means. We have a planet of limited resources which are, for many reasons of history and chance, distributed unevenly and unfairly around the globe, but we should seek to live within these resources. Most reasonably educated and enlightened people would now agree that '*sustainability*' is at the very least a good idea. The problem seems to be that everyone feels it is something that doesn't apply to them. Yet when we destroy the environment we are robbing the next and future generations of the chance to enjoy and to benefit from that unique resource. If you expect the peoples of, say, the Amazon, or of West Africa, for example, to care for and to nurture the environmental resource there, then it seems reasonable to expect the same here in South Yorkshire or the Peak. Yet time and again we simply fail to do this at even the most basic level. Let's take, as an example, Oakes Park in south Sheffield and formerly in Derbyshire. It is a uniquely interesting landscape with the richest neutral grassland in the region. This is a rich resource of fantastic hay meadows and pastures because of the way the landowners, the Bagshaw family, had managed it for around 300 years. It is recognised and designated as a '*Site of Scientific Interest*', and holds good numbers of specially protected and increasingly vulnerable wildlife species. Not only this, but it is a hugely important link in the '*Green Corridor*' designated between the Moss Valley to the south and the urbanised Gleadless Valley to the north. This is the route back into the city for animals such as Badger and most recently Brown Hare, and also deer species. When tenure at the Oakes became less attractive to the family, the land was sold off for development, and the house and stables separated into two different residential development initiatives. Now, a couple of decades and several planning and public enquiries later, the landscape and wildlife, and indeed the unique historic heritage of the site are

still under threat. Nobody will do anything to safeguard or conserve what is one of the region's most valuable assets and it has become '*the elephant in the room*'. There is not a single organisation in the City that has lifted a finger to help conserve this site, and local authority officers and others simply ignore requests for either help or advice. In theory the area is protected by the legislation to safeguard unimproved grassland, but as noted earlier this amounts to a toothless tiger.

Grange Farm at Norton Oakes abandoned and derelict. © Ian Rotherham

But now here's the twist. The bulk of the site has for many years been owned by one of Sheffield's biggest and most successful businesses. You would think that they would be able, willing and committed to conserving this for the people of Sheffield and for posterity. But no, they are deafeningly silent. They even sold off the southern half of the site to an individual householder who then proceeded to plough it all up. Under both the European legislation and the UK law to implement this, the act was totally illegal. But now enter stage left the fat cat judge and the weak-kneed agency officials, with the '*not my job guv'nor attitude*'. The rest is, as they say, history. Yet it is worthwhile considering the detail of this and the attitudes that underlie it, since they have a resonance with much that is wrong with the way in which we disregard the environment and the needs and rights of future generations. Even when the legislation is there to help protect these irreplaceable areas for future generations and for all our benefits, very often ways are found to fail us yet again. The individual responsible apparently claimed that ploughing up many hectares of ancient unimproved orchid meadow was in fact just an extension to his garden as a play area for the kids. On hearing this news Defra, the Government department responsible at the time for overseeing the protection of these areas, stated that in that case it was okay. It was no longer their responsibility. However, this is a Green Belt agricultural site and a change of use to a garden is a change which requires planning permission. Defra, bless them, said it was no longer their responsibility and no, they would not be informing the Planning Authority of the issue. The Planning Authority here is Sheffield City Council, and despite several requests for an opinion as to the legality of the change of land-use, nothing was forthcoming. In several cases officers simply failed to respond to correspondence. So in short, if this was a change of land use then it required Planning Consent and without this there was a serious breach of the legislation. If there was no change of land use then there was a serious breach of the environmental legislation on land improvement, and so Defra would be obliged to step in. Despite many emails, telephone calls, and letters, and months of waiting, no action of any sort was taken. *'Not my job guv'nor'*.

At the same time the Christian Holiday Community at the Oakes, again with zero community consultation, and in the absence of any environmental impact assessment, decided themselves to carry out major works to level and landfill areas around the old house and the historic garden. This did at last generate some belated activity by Planning Officers, but really much too little and much too late. Considerable damage has once again been done. The explanation by the Oakes Centre to local people was that their work wasn't against the law so it was okay. So hardly a shining example of responsible action then; as it happened, it did require an environmental assessment and planning consent was granted retrospectively.

But surely both the individual householder responsible for the damage, and indeed the Christian Holiday Community at the Oakes itself should take a more responsible attitude in the first instance? Isn't this what sustainable development and environmental responsibility and equity are all about? In cases like this, those who have caused such appalling environmental

damage could easily have what they want and need AND do some long-term good as well. They just need to open their eyes to the wider community and environmental need. After all, this is a small planet and we all depend on it. It is therefore in all of our interests to manage it as best we can today and into the future. Surely too, such a big and successful business as the one that owns or has owned the bulk of Oakes Park, could do a little more to provide a sustainable and high quality environment for the people and the wildlife of our region? It seems that we lack vision, commitment, and compassion. We have the means but we simply fail to apply them meaningfully.

Selling our heritage by the pound – the strange case of Abbeydale Hall

If you look around the world and then focus back in on our region, you have a view of the potential and the needs of people and their environment. In recent years it has become even clearer that a good healthy environment makes for a good healthy community; it even helps to enhance peoples' quality of life and they really are often fitter and healthier. You might think this is common sense but it is only when we can scientifically prove it that politicians and decision-makers begin to recognise the obvious. Not only this, but we can now show that a good quality environment also makes a major contribution to a vibrant local and regional economy. It is also now very clear that the old Sheffield adage of *'where there's muck there's brass'* no longer applies. A dirty and polluted environment was once a marker of economic activity and hence wealth, and was acceptable to wealthy industrialists as long as they lived up-wind in the nice western suburbs. Now, a degraded environment is one of the major barriers to inward economic investment and regional economic growth. Yet we still seem to treat the environment as a luxury and an add-on, which is at best an inconvenience to the economy. Of course we don't actually say this, but we disguise the approach in those Weasel-words. Many developments will make claims of being low carbon, energy-efficient, and *'green'*, yet in reality doing little to make any meaningful contribution to environmental quality or a functioning regional ecology. As a friend of mine said back in the early 1990s, the problem is that those damaging the environment have stolen our clothes and our language. So every development, good or bad, will make the same exaggerated claims for benefits to the community and the environment. Sadly, in most cases the reality falls very short. What's worse is that they describe everything as environmentally-friendly and even sustainable, when in reality all they are talking about are a few token gestures on energy and perhaps re-cycling. It has little or nothing to do with the *living* environment.

Surely one of the key issues and really one of the most positive ways forward is through education. This is something I have always believed, and through education we can change the world. I think that is why my final comment on a bad example of lack of conservation and needless environmental damage is so depressing and so poignant.

Field Scabious. © Ian Rotherham

At Abbeydale Hall, an eighteenth century minor hall in south-west Sheffield, there was a wonderful environmental studies centre and adult education base, and set in this historic landscape an award-winning wildlife garden. This was owned by us, the Sheffield public, and the garden was the stepping stone for the Hallam and then Sheffield Conservation Volunteers (now BTCV). All was happy in the garden. Not only that, but the local community was fully involved and raised several thousand pounds for improvement works and even got grants from the then National Rivers Authority (now Environment Agency) to carry out works to improve the stream and the ponds. The site

was scheduled and protected as a '*Community Wildlife Area*' in the *Sheffield Nature Conservation Strategy*, and there was free and open access to the site for the visiting public. At this time, of course, the site and the buildings were owned by Sheffield City Council on behalf of us, the local community. However, in stepped the last Conservative Government with its *Education Act* to devolve educational institutions from their parent local authorities; and lo and behold, the site and the buildings were now owned not by you and me, but by Sheffield College. This was via its Norton College campus. Believe it or not, a major educational body charged with engendering awareness and community spirit amongst its charges and preparing them as active citizens for the future then took the centre at Abbeydale on the most amazing U-turn. Clearly scenting the heady smell of a lot of money if the site and buildings were to be sold off, that is exactly what the College proceeded to do. I fully understand the economics behind this and indeed the pressures of financial constraints in the education sector, but, and it is a big BUT, this was '*our*' asset and not theirs to sell. In a series of very underhand measures the College made it increasingly difficult for the Friends of Abbeydale Hall Wildlife Garden, the ones who for ten years or more had raised funds for, and carried out management of, the award-winning Wildlife Garden, to even visit the site. Eventually the Group were barred from access and even the joint management and liaison committee between the College staff at the Abbeydale Centre and a representative from Norton College Campus was suspended. None of this was in any way democratic and most of it was decidedly underhand. But now with the Friends Group banned from the site and no educational groups allowed to use the fantastic facilities on offer, the College could move swiftly towards their final aim. The site and the buildings were closed as an educational base, ending many decades of vibrant teaching use, and the scene was set for sale and development. The heady scent of filthy lucre was drifting between Abbeydale and Norton.

Pipistrelle Bat. © Ian Rotherham

There was still a barrier to the achievement of the core aim of selling the assets so deviously acquired and then capitalising on the revenue and that was it needed planning consent plus a buyer. The saga ran for quite a while and I'll not bore you here with the details, but eventually a private developer was found, and the important heritage landscape around the front of the Hall was sacrificed to new urban dwellings, and the Hall itself converted to desirable apartments; a simple case of education out and cash flow in. In granting planning consent *AGAINST* the recommendations of the Planning Officers, the then Lib-Dem Councillors of the time had little knowledge of the issues. When questioned, one local Councillor stated that he knew nothing of any conservation or heritage issues and therefore the proposals should go-ahead. Yet the site was an award-winning educational Wildlife Garden and scheduled and protected under the Council's owned strategies as a '*Community Wildlife Area*'.

However, this did leave the problem of the now abandoned Wildlife Garden, which was excluded from the development but from which the public and the Friends Group were now banished. The story carries on today and the landowner still seeks to build on it, this time in 2008, four detached houses. The current Lib-Dem Council finally turned this application down, and well done to the current Planners and the Councillors for speaking up for the local environment. But in many ways the scene was set back in the 1990s, and the bigger damage has already been done. I worry about the role of the College in all this if these are the people responsible with providing educational and hopefully ethical guidance to the next generation. How on earth can we hope to

encourage young people to care for others and to see the world as a precious resource on which we all depend, and for which sustainable development is the only way forwards? Their role models of the adults are giving such a clear message of '*we don't give a damn as long as the price is right*'. Sustainable development is all about equity between people and the environment and especially between communities across the planet, and between generations through time. The latter we describe as '*inter-generational equity*', and is basically that you shouldn't take today what others might need or wish to use and benefit from tomorrow. Abbeydale Hall and its Wildlife Garden should have been celebrated as a '*beacon*' of excellence in promoting environmental awareness and opportunity. With its purpose-built and publicly-funded nature trail for the less able, and some very good interpretational materials already produced, here was an opportunity for the College to be genuinely embedded in the local community and in supporting a sustainable environment. This was a genuine and much needed educational opportunity and a superb role-model for our younger people. But no, '*take the money and run, and to hell with the consequences*' is the only educational message from this shabby story; a pity really. Just after all this went through back in the 1990s, I did spot the Norton College Vice-Principle of the time who had chaired the meetings with the Friends Group. I suspect he was just the messenger in all this, but he did look terribly guilty as he avoided my eyes across the supermarket checkout and slunk away.

Education, education, education

Despite the appalling situation at Abbeydale Hall, and the disappointment all that involved, I still believe that education is the key, and at every level in society. I also feel that at the end of the day, it is individuals that change the world and that we all have a role to play. Some years ago I was sat in my favourite pub, *The Grouse at Longshaw*, and a young lady approached me to ask if I was indeed Ian Rotherham. Having reluctantly admitted to being me, she said how a guided walk at Abbeydale Hall Wildlife Garden many years ago (I think she was seven or eight years old at the time) had helped trigger her interest in, and excitement about, nature and wildlife. She had gone on to get a degree and now worked at quite a senior level with the British Trust for Conservation Volunteers. To me that is what it is all about and why I remain optimistic and hopeful that despite the bully-boys and the double-speak, we can and indeed must prevail. Education is a bit like the drip-drip-drip of water falling on a rock and eroding it away, every little, no matter how seemingly insignificant, must make a difference.

So what do I mean by education? I certainly don't just imply formal study and training. No, I really mean something that is to do with everyone from a '*little tiny*', to senior citizens, and it is to do with enthusing and sharing excitement and interest about wildlife and nature, and then a shared concern for the environment and the future of our rather small planet. Somehow we need to reconnect to our shared roots and to rediscover our ecological core. Technology and economics have muddied the waters and seem to separate us physically and spiritually from nature.

The Gleadless Valley Wildlife Group and friends, 1980s.

We are hooked into a consumer whirlpool that threatens to drag us down into an impoverished existence which simply cannot be sustained. This is just my view, of course, and I don't wish to seem negative. We must be positive and we must seek to rediscover richness in our world and to safeguard this for now and for the future. In doing this, every single individual has a role and a vital part to play. It is not marginal and peripheral to economics or to politics; it is absolutely central and critical to survival. I'm just surprised that politicians and economists don't recognise this, because it

seems to me to be commonsense. The first stage on the way to positive action to halt the decline in the environment and the appalling losses of wildlife and wildlife habitats is to rediscover and to enjoy the natural world around us. I hope that in a small way the newspaper column and the radio show together help to bring this about. If all they achieve is to encourage people across our region to look again at the ecology and heritage that surrounds them and to treasure it a little more, then it will have been worthwhile.

My annual 'spring' birdwatch in the Gleadless Valley, 1980s. © Ian Rotherham

I've been actively engaged and involved in teaching since the early 1980s, and unfortunately through this time witnessed the ravages of Thatcherite politics on my sort of education. When I began we had adult education, what was called '*liberal studies*' provided by the Local Education Authority, the Worker's Educational Association, and by Sheffield University. The WEA still provides classes purely for enjoyment, but the others have gone by the wayside. Everything today has to be audited and it has to pay its way immediately and directly by cash. This is a real shame and as a community and a society it is a huge step backwards. It is great to get adult education courses that allow students to get a qualification, as happens with the Centre for Lifelong Learning now at Sheffield University. But we have lost the potential to study just for pleasure and for its own sake. In losing this we have lost a great number of other benefits too. It was through collaborations between these three providers in the 1980s that we established programmes of training and activities which set up, for example, the region's first local Wildlife group, the Moss Valley Wildlife Group. With education projects managed by the LEA's then environmental education tutor, Oliver Blensdorf, we ran courses and even had weekend training based at Northern College on aspects of conservation and even environmental politics. The Moss Valley Wildlife Group subsequently defeated Sheffield City Council at the Green Belt Enquiry – something of a first even at a national level. The outcomes included the setting up of a fully funded countryside service for the valley and a Wildlife Group that is still active today. Similar patterns happened in Gleadless Valley with the establishment and training of a local group, and now the designation of Local National Reserve status and a fully constituted conservation trust. The project has generated, amongst other things, grant aid to the area totalling many tens of thousands of pounds over the last twenty years. This is not a bad achievement for just a few hundred pounds initial investment. The same happened in the Shire Brook Valley in south-east Sheffield but with massive grant aid drawn down to establish a nature reserve and educational facilities. Yet today it would be very hard indeed to support a community-led initiative such as this.

A shared enthusiasm.

The important trigger of the first few classes and the initial steps towards confidence for local people to survey and to then manage their own environment would be hard indeed with current funding and provision models for education. There are many other benefits and too much to discuss here. But local people of all ages, and especially the older and retired individuals and couples gain enormously and I'm sure it improves both physical and mental health. The groups and bonds formed are very beneficial to individuals and to society and help in developing inter-generational links within an

area too. Another important outcome from such groups is the fostering and exchanging and often documenting of local memories and local histories. Without the seed-corn investment in education for enjoyment, and at a price which all can easily afford, none of these other benefits flow. Sure there are now ways of raising funds such as through the National Lottery, but these don't generate the initial confidence to develop a project and to submit a funding package. Most of our local projects and initiatives grew from low-cost educational provision; the benefits still flow today.

Wildlife watching is a great way to meet and share.

Memories of Abbeydale Hall Wildlife Garden in the early 1990s

I'm sitting on one of the rough-sawn log benches recently provided by the Conservation Volunteers based here. It is a summer evening and all the volunteers have gone home; some across Sheffield and others further afield across South Yorkshire. The local '*friends*' live just around the corner. Around a hundred yards away is one of Sheffield's busy arterial roads, the Abbeydale Road South, full of hustle and bustle. The other side of the Garden is Sheffield Club, the leading Rugby Union Club in the area. This is very much the suburban residential zone of a big city. The old Hall was built maybe in the early 1700s with bits added on and knocked about ever since. It has an air of calm and tranquillity, of time everlasting linked to a deep-seated past and a long future. This really is an amazing oasis for wildlife and for people. The recent work on clearing silt has opened up the water on main pond and the Moorhens are nesting close by the over-hanging old Yews. All the disabled access routes have now been completed and interpretation boards showing the species around the garden are done and erected. Along with all this the butterfly and bee garden is all a-buzz. Today we've had good numbers of Small Tortoiseshell, Peacock, Red Admiral and even the less abundant Comma. There's a heady fragrance of Honeysuckle rescued from the bulldozers when they ripped out some ancient woodlands along the route of the Stocksbridge By-pass. The Garden now has a woodland bank with Bluebells, Greater Stitchwort, Wood Anemone, Wood Melick Grass, Foxgloves, Primroses and others; all rescued and now hopefully all in a permanent home. With everyone else gone, I can sit here and wait. There's a Grey Heron prospecting overhead and hoping to come down to take fish or Frogs, but it has seen me and thinks better of it. The Great Spotted Woodpecker, however, is nesting close-by and isn't too worried about me. There's the hallmark high-pitched *chik chik* call, but otherwise he's more intent on feeding the increasingly demanding youngsters. Earlier in the day we had a glimpse of the local Kingfisher, here looking for easy fish, but nesting back down on the River Sheaf a quarter of a mile away. Now as the evening creeps in the bats are prospecting around the buildings and across the pond. I've seen a couple of the larger Noctule Bats flying quite high over the site earlier on, but now it is the tiny Pipistrelles, fluttering round the lower trees and out over the open water. I can just about hear their sonic calls; almost a high-pitched scratching or churring sound. This ability to hear high-pitched sounds is something you lose with age, and men lose earlier than women. But my hearing must still be okay as I can make these out pretty well, but then they are now coming just a few feet from my head. Around the magnificent larger trees here I can see but not hear two, maybe three, Brown Long-eared Bats. Their echo-locating is quieter and hence the need for their disproportionately long ears. They tend to fly close in to the tree canopy too. I'm hoping for the Water Bat or Daubenton's Bat, but I suspect that the pond here is too small. Just down the road at Tyzack's Dam, the mill pond for Abbeydale Industrial Hamlet, we get them almost every night. I'm staying late this evening because tomorrow we have an open day and a bat walk. (This event actually draws a crowd of over a hundred people of all ages from tiny tots to grandparents and from a very wide area). Tonight I'm checking what we might expect, though the Bat activity depends so much on the prevailing weather conditions. We need a nice sultry warm and humid evening with little wind and lots of big fat-bodied moths. So as ten pm draws near I'm preparing to leave when a Tawny Owl floats out of the darkness like an enormous moth and lands in the dead tree opposite me. I freeze with anticipation and hardly daring to breathe. It rotates its enormous head as owls do, and I can just about make out its large, dark eyes. Then with silent wings, but the typical *huick huick* call, it rises up and away to where its youngsters are calling, sat out on the roof-top of the old Hall. As I turn to leave I disturb a rather large Fox, out looking for Voles and Wood Mice. He's not too fazed and lopes off like a small rangy Wolf and through a gap in the hedge into the neighbouring gardens. What a nice way to finish my evening. I just hope that tomorrow, when we do the walk, it will be as good.

Above: Newfield Spring Wood in the Moss Valley bulldozed by a grant-aided 'sensitive management scheme' in the 1980s; paid for by us!
Below: ancient woodland near Stocksbridge bulldozed to make way for the by-pass. No environmental assessment was done here. Some of the ancient woodland wild flowers were rescued and taken to a safe sanctuary. Guess where? Abbeydale Hall Wildlife Garden. Both photographs © Ian Rotherham

THE WILD SIDE OF SHEFFIELD AND THE PEAK

The Peak District moors at Froggatt Edge in winter. © Ian Rotherham

Urban Otters and Knotweed Jungles in South Yorkshire

In sharp contrast to the above image, the industrial lowlands paint a very different picture. Yet there is wildlife aplenty along the urban rivers. The view across the urban, industrial River Don is surprising – a blunt, brown nose just shows through dense vegetation giving away the secret; an Otter. Always good to see but this is even more exciting; an urban Otter back in town. It is amazing when the river was biologically dead only thirty years ago. I've seen Water Voles and Water Shrews here and in good numbers, but recently Mink have arrived. This American cousin of the Otter (both in the Weasel family) spread throughout Britain after releases from fur farms, a threat to native wildlife, especially Water Voles. Local fishermen here see more Mink and fewer Voles. If you track further up towards and beyond Deepcar you'll find an unspoilt river that looks like it could be in the heart of a Scottish glen; a clean trout river with

all the wildlife that implies. Here, if you quietly crouch and wait, there's a good chance of the Dipper; bouncing up and down, or flying low, piping loudly as it establishes and defends its territory. The South Yorkshire Pennine-fringe is good habitat for these nationally-uncommon birds. Acid rain threatened them a few years ago but they seem to have recovered. You'll also see the Grey Heron, and even the fish-eating duck, the Goosander. The latter is a real show-off, the males having pinkish-white breasts and flanks, and a metallic green head.

But back in the urban heartland, calling loudly a Kingfisher flies past; nesting nearby in an old industrial drain-pipe in the river's concrete and brick retaining walls. With a Grey Heron drifting heavily and lazily past our vantage-point, it confirms recovery in this urban ecology; ten or more fish species back in our river, including trout. This is one ecosystem making remarkable progress. Perhaps the Otters will oust the Mink

23

and the Voles will thrive again too. Careful examination of the recently-wet mud on the lower riverbank confirms the presence of Deer, probably Red. Increasingly though, it will be worth looking out for signs of Roe Deer too, or even the secretive alien, the Muntjac. With a high-pitched jangling rattle, a glance up reveals a Grey Wagtail perhaps anxious that I'm too close to its nest, or maybe it's just showing off! So as I move quietly away, scrambling back up the steep bank, there is a sudden screaming and flurry of high-velocity activity close over my head: the Devil Bird! Well actually it's a group of Swifts recently arrived and proclaiming their patch very excitedly. This is the bird that for me says summer is on its way. It is also a very urban bird and so a bit special. Although they're not exactly rare, they are localised; and they depend on artificial structures, particularly old buildings. So if rows of terraced houses are demolished, and the new buildings don't provide for Swifts, then the population could plummet. The loss of the cockney Sparrow is a warning that we must heed, and it's down to planners and developers to save the day.

Himalayan Balsam. © Ian Rotherham

I used to walk through Meersbrook Park in order to cross the City to King Edwards School. In early summer hundreds of Swifts wheeled around my head, sometimes so close you could feel the brush of their wings. I wonder if they still do. My childhood memories were forged by such experiences, and the trip was followed by the pungent smell, of Tyzacks' Works with its over-powering vinegary odour, then the heady sweetness of the mint-rock factory, and chlorine from Heeley Baths, and the not-infrequent pong

of a sewage overflow too; the rich experience of Sheffield's urban countryside as I crossed the River Sheaf!

It was here too, that I first saw Himalayan Balsam and Japanese Knotweed. Very soon during the summer heat the air will be heavy with the pungent fragrance of exotic Balsam. The Otters will lie-up in the dense riverside vegetation of alien Japanese Knotweed. Now superabundant along many urban rivers, Knotweed causes huge environmental problems, and conservationists are keen to control, if not eradicate. Yet on the urban river, dense Knotweed, established as industrial pollution declined, provides wonderful cover to allow wildlife back into city heartlands. Now there's a thought.

Yarncliff Wood, Peak District

Bluebell carpets gave a heady atmosphere to May's ancient woods; evocative wild places, linked in our psyche to primeval wild forest. Yet they are not as they seem. People lived and worked in them over past centuries. But we love myth, and reality shouldn't intervene too deeply, Oak and Bluebell are symbolic of lost wilderness and maybe lost innocence. Yarncliff Wood near Fox House is ancient oakwood hanging in a steep gritstone gorge, hewn from the rock by waters swollen after the last Ice Age. Today's stream is more modest. The old Oaks are wizened, multi-stemmed medusas, from centuries as coppice wood for charcoal. This finished here in the late 1700s or early 1800s, but walk down the valley, north of the stream, and evidence of long-disused charcoal hearths tells the story. Several metres across, these oval platforms were levelled with a down-slope edge or a small wall of medium-sized boulders. Charcoal burners placed short lengths of cut coppice called cordwood in carefully-designed stacks a couple of metres high. Finally covered by turf and soil from the woodland floor, with vegetation and other debris, the stack was set alight to burn slowly over two days. Hard, dirty work, it needed constant supervision. Like many British crafts this tradition died out almost completely by the 1950s. Recently revived for demonstration over here, it still occurs in Eastern

Europe and the Mediterranean. Walk in any ancient woodland in the UK and you follow the footsteps of former workers and craftsmen.

Padley Gorge and Yarncliff in late May or early June offer many other delights as the Bluebells fade into memory. Look down and the ground is covered by large Red Wood Ants. On still, hot days you can hear the leaves and ground rustling with their activity. It's best not to sit down! With the ants comes a host of associated wildlife. You'll hear the laughing call of the Green Woodpecker, or aptly named 'Yaffle'. This used to be one of the few places to see them in our area, but they've spread. I hear them at Oakes Park, and you've a good chance on former colliery sites like Grimethorpe in Barnsley or down Stone Lane in the Shire Book Valley, Sheffield. I remember a neighbour seeing one at the bottom of Warminster Road in Norton Lees, Sheffield. We all thought it was parrot; but then I was about five years old.

Ancient Oak coppice at Yarncliff Wood, Padley. © Ian Rotherham

Back at Yarncliff watch out for the rare Wood Warbler as this is a good place for them. Also, and often in the better woodland habitats there are Common Redstarts (which aren't really very common anymore), a stunning cousin of the Robin. And here, too, there is an excellent chance of Pied Flycatchers. My spy from Froggatt tells me it is a good year for this summer visitor. They love nest-boxes and he has around twelve in use in woodland not far away. Occasionally they have turned up in urban gardens as far east as Walkley in Sheffield. They do pass through the entire area on migration and especially in August can be seen all along the

east coast. However, in terms of breeding they are really a western oakwood species, and our eastern population is very significant. We are at about the south-eastern limit of the breeding distribution. This is a very pretty bird and the male in particular is a brilliant black and white show-off!

If you can hang around Padley into the late evening then there's a good chance of mammals such as Badger, Fox and even Red Deer. The best thing is to sit tight and wait quietly. This becomes more difficult in a few weeks because of the midges. You'll soon have various bat species flying close over your head, but don't try to identify them; that's for the experts. With any luck a Tawny Owl or two should keep you entertained, and hopefully a Badger or Fox will make an appearance. A still, warm evening is often best. This is a special place and it is a special time; so make the most of it. When all's done you can wend your way back, via the Grouse Inn at Froggatt to enjoy local hospitality too. Now that's a good day out!

It's hot, hot, and getting hotter in and around Sheffield

I'm sure one of the 'happenings' of the 2006 summer was the hot weather. We were pretty much sweltering for weeks; despite the rain this is set to last for years to come. There are many arguments as to the causes and possible problems, plus what, if anything, we can do about it. I suggest that if you really want to depress yourself try a holiday read of 'Global Catastrophes – A Very Short Introduction' by Bill McGuire (Oxford University Press). This cheerily introduces what is happening to our planet and its implications now and in the future. Anyone with children or grandchildren should take time out to read this. Remember the famous environmental truth that 'We do not inherit the Earth – we borrow it from our descendants'. Then cast around our region and see what we do and how seriously we take the issues and responsibilities. We are doing some good things but (a big BUT) we are also doing a lot wrong. Let me know about your neighbourhood, both good and bad. I'm starting this week with my own patch in Norton, Sheffield, just to get the ball rolling. My experience does not give cause for optimism. Our local wildflower meadow in Oakes Park, in the Green Belt, full of orchids and butterflies was recently ploughed up. It is now, according to the owner, an extension to his back garden. That this is an historic site and a scheduled *Site of Scientific Interest* is forgotten in the rush to level it as a play area – personal gain at the expense of the local community and wildlife. Interestingly two big reports have come out recently highlighting massive declines of butterflies and moths across Britain. These describe the impacts of the increasingly hot weather and the effects of habitat destruction and neglect, placing my local site in a bigger picture. Scaled up across the region, the UK and the planet, we are not borrowing from our children but flogging the family silver like there's no tomorrow. Close by at the Oakes Park Hall, are run educational holidays, and Sheffield City Council recently issued a *Stop Notice* to prevent further damage to the historic park with diggers and earth-movers levelling the ridge-and-furrow grasslands and disrupting the boundaries of the listed historic garden. It really shouldn't happen. English Heritage and the local archaeology services have been notified and we await responses; (still waiting in 2008!) It gets worse, with a local sports club north of the Park tipping rubbish into the ancient trackway carpeted with Bluebells and other woodland wildflowers, supposedly protected locally and nationally. Bluebell is a target species for the *Sheffield Local Biodiversity Action Plan*, yet over two years have passed since this was reported to the City Council and to interested groups, but nothing gets done. Each year a little more of the woodland and hedgerow habitat disappears. I'm sure that if Bluebells could read they would be reassured by the official plan to protect them!

Not far away in Graves Park, the wildflower meadows were notified as *Sites of Scientific Interest* back in the early 1990s. They received national media coverage when management, led by the late Dr Oliver Gilbert and myself, produced abundant flowers like Pignut and Field Scabious, clouds of Blue and Brown Butterflies, and a number of orchid species. You would hope and maybe assume that Sheffield City Council, knowing the importance of their historic landscape, dedicated for public good by Alderman Graves, would have a plan of action in accord with their own policies and *Local Biodiversity Action Plans*. But again no; the area is mismanaged and neglected. Abandoned wildflower meadows grow tall and rank, bad for most wildlife; and other areas have trees planted on them. No doubt this was well intentioned, but unique and precious wildlife sites are threatened. In other parts of Sheffield, nearby Gleadless Valley, Loxley Valley, or Shire Brook for example, there are excellent conservation projects in place attracting grant aid and other support, and growing local jobs. So I wonder what is wrong with my patch and why nobody seems to care. How does it feel in your part of the world?

Big Issues but Big Opportunities too

Well, two weeks away and time to put my feet up and relax, and to read the newspapers. Hmmm. Some of the headlines are not exactly cheerful, even if we disregard international affairs, terrorism, war, *etc*. Recent copies of national newspapers included the following headlines: '*Tigers on the brink of extinction*'; '*Take the money or safeguard the land; plans for world's biggest windfarm divide Lewis*'; '*Earth facing catastrophic loss of species*'; *Drought, gales and refugees; what will happen as UK hots up*'; and then of particular interest as I'm swimming with a couple of large jellyfish off the Cornish coast, '*Invasion of the warm-water aliens*'. It certainly makes you think and I was up the beach and thumbing through a field guide to check if my jellyfish were serious stingers or just a little bit naughty. The guidance was a bit vague and ranged from '*they sting*' for some species to '*serious, dangerous, and avoid; please alert the coastguard*'. I can take a hint and self-preservation is a strong instinct, so best avoid! But jellyfish off the coast will be the least of our problems as things hot up. Frankly it can all seem a bit depressing and makes you think there's not much you can do. Well that isn't the case. It is true that as individuals not many of us can change the World (although we are all doing our bit to warm it up). Yet individuals can and do make a difference. Research by Geoff Cartwright, a colleague at Sheffield Hallam University, showed that the key to successful environmental action was '*project champions*', people that make things happen, that seize opportunities and won't let go. This applies at national and global scales and right down to those in the communities in

Sheffield, Barnsley, Rotherham, and Doncaster, in fact all over the region and often unsung heroes at that.

An invasive 'thug' the American signal Crayfish.
© Peter Wolstenholme

Internationally, individuals like David Bellamy, founder of the national conservation body Plantlife, Sir Peter Scott, founder of the Wildfowl Trust and the World Wildlife Fund (now the Wildfowl and Wetlands Trust, and the Worldwide Fund for Nature), and Sir David Attenborough have changed perceptions, raised awareness, and made things happen. They are project champions for wildlife and the environment. The name Octavia Hill may be less familiar to many readers, but she is someone whose efforts affected everyone in Britain and still do so. Along with a handful of other individuals such as John Ruskin (with a particularly strong association with Sheffield), she developed the ideas and vision behind the National Trust. The movement emerged in the mid 1800s as a reaction to the gross despoilation of nature and of society by industry and by agricultural intensification. One of the final straws was the rapacious enclosure of common land and heaths that displaced the rights of local people and in London took away opportunities for recreation and leisure; private greed and destruction of public benefit. (I'm sure they would have been shocked to see the continuing losses of ancient grasslands and heaths across our region over the last twenty years, and continuing today). A look across the threatened wildflower meadows of Sheffield's Oakes Park confirms that these threats are as active today as they ever were.

However, despite the overwhelming odds and powerful interests opposing them, this group of stalwart Victorians set about changing their world (and ours) for the better. So on January 12th 1895 the National Trust for Places of Historic Interest or Natural Beauty was formally established. What these people did not only changed their lives, but yours too. Many places and landscapes we take for granted today are only there because of these visionaries. Many people across our region visit Longshaw, Kinder Scout, Clumber Park, or Hardwick Hall, just a few of the rich variety of Trust properties around Sheffield. Farther afield, if you've been to the English Lake District or perhaps to the coast this summer, then you will almost certainly have visited Trust land or properties. Now, as one of the most active conservation bodies in the UK, in fact in the World, the Trust employs people, conserves buildings and wildlife, and supports the regeneration of entire rural economies. They've evolved from a far off vision of a few rather eccentric Victorians, to a powerful force for good in a world that is increasingly uncertain and in which we as individuals seem powerless to help. This also makes it easy for you to help the environment and to enjoy it to the full, by joining the Trust. It isn't cheap, but it is excellent value.

It's wet, wet, wet

The good news is that the water is going down; the bad news is it will get worse. Around a decade ago Professor Chris Baines and I proposed, to Sheffield City Council, a detailed study with support from Yorkshire Water and the Environment Agency. The concern was that the impact of land use, both agriculture and increasingly urbanisation, had modified the water catchment (the gathering grounds and floodplains) over decades and centuries. Now, with climate change, the consequences were likely to be increased flooding, both in frequency and in quantity. The response to our short report and presentation was disappointing. They were not interested. The reason given by senior planners was that recent engineering works at the time had resolved Sheffield's water issues. '*There was little point in the study, as Sheffield would not flood again*'. Downstream was not their concern.

River Rother in flood June 2007. © Christine Handley

This is a very complicated problem and so I will keep it brief, to the point, and simple. Inland flooding occurs for two main reasons. First is that the engineered channels (above ground) or drains (below ground) cannot cope. Many in urban areas date from the Victorian townships and are simply too small. This can mean flooding almost anywhere in the system; but obviously you are most likely to get wet downstream or in a bottleneck. There are other complications with different types of sewer and mixing of clean water and foul water, and in summer flash floods the possibility of sewers blocking. I remember standing in the middle of Ecclesall Woods when a storm broke and the stream flooded with raw sewage very suddenly, surprisingly, and very unpleasantly.

The second reason for floods is what we have done to the landscape. Over centuries and increasingly in the last fifty years, we straightened rivers and streams, culverted them, canalised them, and constrained them. In the wider landscape from the high Pennines to the lowland valleys and the great open lands around Doncaster, we have drained, drained, and drained them. Look around the region and every little bit of land is affected. All that concrete and tarmac means rainwater runs off quickly, every roof, and every building contributes to the process. However, most greenspace is drained too: the parks, playing fields, farmers' fields. All our moorlands have '*grips*' that pour the water off. Even the woodlands were drained by the Victorians and then by twentieth century park-keepers. The final nail in the coffin is that the

region, like many parts of Britain, historically had extensive wetlands. These ran from the great Pennine uplands, down the river valleys before spewing out across the lowlands of Doncaster and beyond. The south Yorkshire Fens was the third biggest fenland in England until the Dutch engineers began the drainage of 99% of it in the 1700s. Abercrombie in his seminal report of 1931 [*Sheffield and District Regional Planning Scheme*] noted, '*...the danger of permitting building upon low-lying land, and especially that which is liable to floods. The Minister questions whether public money should be spent in protecting the property of anyone who is so foolish as to build upon such perilous sites.*' The problem is not new. In 1546, the ancient chapel at Attercliffe was still in use so that the curate of Rotherham could come to his flock when it was too wet for them to come to him, or to provide service even when he could not get there! He had '*...to mynistre to the seke people, as when the waters of the Rothere and Downe* (DON) *are so urgent that the curate of Rotherham cannot to them repayre, nor the inhabitants unto hym nether on horseback or bote...*'

Climate change makes this much worse very quickly. We have more water falling on us in doses that are more intensive. It has to go somewhere and engineering alone will not solve it. We suggested a landscape-wide approach to use Nature's own systems to slow the flow, to mop up the water, to hold it back and to dissipate the impacts. It will not solve all the problems. However, is a start and it was suggested over ten years ago. Perhaps now is the time to revisit this idea.

River Rother at Woodhouse Washlands June 2007. © Christine Handley

Spare a thought for our rivers and their wildlife

I have just returned home from visiting the Derbyshire Derwent at Chatsworth. This is our most glorious river and a rich home for many wild animals and plants. I think I saw fewer birds today on the whole of the stretch that I walk than ever before. It was as though the river had been mugged and then left, abandoned. The cause of the problem was nowhere to be seen but the evidence of the crime is all around with piles of mud, debris and detritus, dead trees washed downstream, vegetation on the islands simply swept away by the force of the current. Most striking of all though was the absence of birds, and most worryingly, no youngsters. Have they left, escaping to safer waters, or have they perished in the unexpected onslaught of the summer's flood? Only time will tell, but the omens are not good. There were quite a few Mallards, as always, but mostly adults. The birds are hard to distinguish at this time of year as they go into a major moult called the '*eclipse*', and lose all their colours. A single adult Mute Swan and an accompanying immature floated gracefully in front of the ornamental bridge. However, that was about it. There were a few Sand Martins, but it looked as though some of their nest banks had washed away (which is an annual occurrence, Sand Martins leading a precarious life). Several sites looked as through they had been washed out by the floodwaters. A solitary Dipper flew rather furtively up from the usual site near the old mill, its calls lost in the roar of the waters that still pour over the weir.

Of course, floods are nothing new, they have always happened, but the recent incidents are unusual for their severity and the season. The Derwent has flooded in winter and spring in recent years, and that can be damaging for wildlife. However, the damage is limited by the fact that most plants are dormant at that time, and neither birds nor mammals are breeding. Late spring floods do take a marked toll of waterside breeding birds, but there may be a chance to nest again. At this time of year it is very unlikely, and of course youngsters may be tied to the nest site and unable to escape the inexorable rise of the water. My river at Chatsworth (well actually it is the Duke's, but you know what I mean!), was not particularly badly affected. It was certainly not so bad as the Rother or the Don, so what has happened to the wildlife there? I have heard rumours of Badger setts washed out and abandoned, but what about Water Voles or even Otters. I did see Moorhens on the Don just after the waters went down, so some of the local birds survived, but it looked to me as if all the nests were totally washed away.

Swallowtail Butterfly. © Ian Rotherham

On a happier note, I have started to notice a few butterflies about, and when the sun does get out, it is very hot. This is good for butterflies and for dragonflies and damselflies. Do let me know what you have seen. In my garden, I saw my first hedge brown butterfly this year, and then one warm, slightly humid evening a Swallowtail Moth. It is not to be confused with the ever so rare Swallowtail Butterfly (found only in a handful of East Anglian fens), but a real little beauty nevertheless. For a moth, it is rather large, perhaps 2-3 inches across its wings, and is a pale creamy white, almost ghost-like. It is quite common and will come to windows if you have a light on, and is certainly a moth to look out for. The other wildlife doing rather well with all the rain are slugs and snails which are absolutely everywhere. I even had a willow tree covered in Banded Snails, some several metres off the ground.

Floods and climate - what should we do?

As you might expect, I've had quite a few letters about water and floods. Two in particular struck a chord. Bill Booker of Sheffield 12 wrote in with some really interesting snippets and a copy of a letter or poem from Thomas Booker (Bill's great,

great grandfather – and Bill states that he himself is 77) about the Sheffield Flood in 1864. It is very moving to read the handwriting of somebody who was there at the time. Bill has raised interesting and sensible points about the causes of the floods and the issues that relate to them He asks about the costs of clearing up, about the need to invest in resources and infrastructures too. He also says '*I think it would be foolish, even madness to contemplate building new houses or buildings in the flood zones.*' Well observation would suggest that madness hasn't stopped anybody yet. Bill's letter goes on to advocate the use of recycled materials to reinforce flood banks and other infrastructures of flood defence. This is a theme developed by A.J. Morton of Mexborough, who suggests that we could use materials recycled from former coal sites to create giant flood banks within which the River Don would flow. He apparently saw this when on service with the Forces in Germany, where it was used to control the Rhine. He further feels that this would also help clean up former industrial wastelands, making the old coaling sites suitable for housing. This is a case of killing two birds with one stone.

I can see where both Bill and A.J. are coming from on this, but I do have some doubts. I'm in agreement on the need to be imaginative and to look for new and clever ways to solve long-standing and now immediate problems. I can also see the attractions of freeing up despoiled land and using the material to create huge flood banks to safeguard the land alongside from flooding. So, here are my doubts. One is that over the centuries, and increasingly in recent decades, we have changed the very landscape in which we live, work, and recreate. Our urban areas have spread, spewing out over floodplains, and turning soft, porous surfaces to tarmac and concrete. But we have also drained and 'improved' huge areas of farmland, from the highest parts of the Pennines and the North York Moors, with their 'gripping' drains, to the lowlands of the Vale of York and the flatlands of Doncaster. Driven by government polices over decades, and by massive subsidies from EU and UK governments, we have drained, drained and drained. Rivers have been straightened and

canalised, now locked into artificial banks, the natural drainage systems are de-coupled from their floodplains which are reduced or removed. Alongside the rivers there is intensive farming that increased particularly from the 1950s to the 1990s, especially in flood risk areas such as throughout the Rother Valley and the Don Valley. Then, in recent years we've begun to build anew on the once expansive floodplains, the natural control systems of the region's lowlands. Now, with the extreme weather events dumping unbelievable quantities of water on us in short, intensive periods, but also then continuing with rain over long periods, the system can't cope. With what we have done, this is hardly surprising.

Flooded engineering works along the Rother 1957. From the Environment Agency archive

So what to do? Engineering is one solution but treats symptoms not causes, the *sticking plaster approach*. We need to learn from recent events to '*work with the grain of nature not against it*'. In South Yorkshire, drainage has destroyed around 99% of the South Yorkshire Fens and much moorland has gone or been drained. It is also important to realise that drought and flood are flip-sides of the same problem – you recall that not so long ago Yorkshire had horrendous droughts. All major new developments should adopt sustainable water systems, and key players in the future will be farmers. We need to work with, and pay them, as custodians of the landscape, managing their land to hold back floodwaters. Not cheap, but less costly than repeated damage and disruption, and continued distress and suffering for the region's home-owners and others.

After the floods - some good news stories

We've had tragedies with flooding across South Yorkshire, but I have some more positive reports. Apparently some Badger setts that were washed out have Badgers back. Graham Shepherd of South Yorkshire Badger Group emailed to say '*I visited a sett on the banks of the Don on 2/7/07, a week after the flood. The water had been up about 15ft which is about 2ft above the sett. However one hole had been reopened and the other had clear signs of fresh attempts to clear out the silt, with various footprints easily visible. The possibilities are that the badgers could have swum out, or already out and returned later, or visiting badgers may have come to the sett after the flood.*' That is great news and encouraging for other wildlife affected. Most mammals swim pretty well and cope with localised flooding. There's also a report from Woodseats, Sheffield – a Lapwing nest plus young, clinging to life just above rising floodwater. Still there the next day after the waters went down, they survived.

Woodhouse Washlands Nature Reserve (on the Sheffield/Rotherham border) bore the brunt of severe flooding. Run by the Yorkshire Wildlife Trust it is part of the natural Rother floodplain, just above Catcliffe where much devastation occurred. Interestingly, when we've had flooding here before, locally-rare plants like Yellow Rattle, were carried downstream and appeared on the Nature Reserve the year after. This is one way that plants that are uncommon today used to get around when floods were regular. Another method in the old days was via cow or sheep '*poo*', as animals moved between hay meadows and pastures of local farms. It was obviously ready fertilised, but we can pass over the details. The Washlands Reserve is recovering well, and Nature Reserve Chair, Christine Handley reports good numbers of dragonflies and damselflies turning up. This can be a cracking site for these, with several big species now starting to show. You really want a good, hot, humid day with no wind. Then look out for Emperor Dragonflies (huge with a long blue body) and the hawkers – Northern (up on the moors and rather greenish in colour), and in the lower areas, including some gardens, either Southern Hawker (slightly smaller and generally blue and black), or Migrant Hawker (similar but

smaller still). There are other medium-sized species, and lots of smaller cousins of the dragons, the damselflies. These are generally quite difficult to identify. They mostly hold their wings lengthwise along their body (the abdomen) when at rest. In contrast, the dragons' wings stick straight out. Woodhouse Washlands has had nearly twenty species of dragons and damsels, and most of these have bred. Flying fast, with many species similar in appearance, they are not easy for the beginner to identify. But if you are interested, then get along to a meeting of your local natural history society or local Wildlife Trust and they will help you. Quite a few country parks and nature reserves organise public events and walks to introduce people to the region's dragons and damsels. It is good fun so go along and try it.

Upland special: the Golden Ringed Dragonfly. © Ian Rotherham

Just returning to the theme of Badgers, I had a fantastic view of a young one feeding by the roadside out at Houndkirk Moor, west of Whirlow in Sheffield. This was about half past ten at night, and it was hoovering up what appeared to be a very large earthworm. Those who know Badgers may be familiar with the fact that earthworms form a sizeable part of their diet. I haven't tried one, but they are full of protein (apparently). Even stranger though, was an anecdote from my neighbour Mike Plant, about a friend of his feeding Badgers in south Sheffield. They are coming into his garden, which is now not that uncommon in the region, and feasting every evening. The interesting thing though is what they are eating. I know Badgers love peanuts, and they also like cat food or dog food left out for them. But no, what these are eating is buttered bread, and it has to be with good quality butter, not margarine!

Wildlife with the 'Wow Factor'

Some wildlife species have '*the wow factor*'; important in grabbing people's attention and getting support for nature conservation. Internationally these would include Giant Pandas and Tigers, for example. Closer to home the Waxwing, a stunning wintertime visitor from northern Europe, is also one. With exotic looks, not only does the Waxwing make a wonderful, high-pitched, trilling call, but key to impressing passers-by, it is very approachable. This is important and we'll come back to Waxwings later in the year. However, this week I want to share with you one of my other favourite birds with wow factor in a very big way. In fact it is fair to say that this is a bird with serious style. I'm talking about the Red Kite. This impressive bird of prey is becoming a familiar sight across Britain. Male and female Red Kite are similarly coloured; the female slightly larger than the male. The name '*Kite*' is from the Anglo-Saxon '*cyta*' and historically it had a number of local names such as '*Glead*' or '*Gleade*'. Gleadless in Sheffield for example, is '*the clearing of the Red Kite*'. The '*Puttock*' is another name used in Shakespeare's time. Other names are descriptively *Swallow Buzzard*, or *Whistling Kite*; the latter referring to its distinctive call. It was once a common sight in medieval towns and cities, so much so that Shakespeare described London as a '*city of kites and crows*'. Indeed Red Kites were valued scavengers helping keep streets clean (I wonder if Streetforce know this?) and even protected by Royal decree – killing one was potentially a capital offence. Breeding Red Kites were lost from Yorkshire in the early 1800s and the last English ones from Lincolnshire in 1870-1871, and from Scotland in 1879. Apart from a pair nesting in Devon in 1913, and in Cornwall in 1920, that was it. The Kite hung on, but in decreasing numbers and only in central Wales. So you might think why am I writing about this magnificent bird? Well it is because they are back with us, and after an absence of nearly 200 hundred years this is wonderful news.

Red Kite. From a Victorian print

The RSPB have recently reported the situation in our region, with one of the reintroduction sites set up at Harewood House. They have described the progress of one particular individual called *Scarlet*, released in 2004 as part of the Northern Kites Project in the Derwent Valley near Gateshead. During her short life, she's visited the Chilterns and Wales before deciding that Yorkshire was the place to set up home. We know this because Scarlet, carries pink/yellow identification wing tags, and she has a radio transmitter so Red Kite project staff and volunteers can track her travels. After a long journey through England and Wales, she's headed into Yorkshire to settle down and raise a family. Pairing with a male from the Yorkshire Red Kite Project, they have this summer raised two youngsters at a secret nest east of Harrogate. Scarlet and her mate are one of thirty-six pairs of Red Kites which have raised seventy-five chicks in Yorkshire this year. Interestingly, Doug Simpson, the Red Kite Co-ordinator, said: '*We think there may be even more successful breeding pairs elsewhere in the county which may not have been traced.*' In fact there are hundreds of areas which are potentially suitable for the birds to breed, making it difficult to locate them all; so definitely worth looking out for across the region. Red Kites like scattered woodland with farmland and grassland nearby. Scarlet was named by schoolchildren in Gateshead as part of the Northern Kites '*adopt-a-kite project*', and news of her progress and photographs of her chicks at the nest were passed to the youngsters. This really is a great way to get kids, parents and staff involved in wildlife conservation, but of course it has taken a huge amount of planning, of enthusiasm and of money. The Yorkshire Red Kite Project began in 1999 with twenty-one birds from the Chilterns released at Harewood near Leeds. By 2003, sixty-nine birds had been released and were established as a thriving population. Wouldn't it be nice to get a population established closer to home, at say Chatsworth?

Roe deer. © Paul Hobson

The Merlin

It seems like Kestrels are doing well this year. I saw at least five over the motorway verge on the M18/M1 intersection last week. I presume they were a family that had fledged early, although I'd normally expect them a couple of weeks from now. Perhaps this is another reflection of the warmer weather and earlier springs. Anyway

it was good to see, since Kestrels were reported to be having problems the last year or so. This is probably our most familiar bird of prey, with its typical '*windhover*' behaviour known to all. It is the one species that still hung on despite the impacts of pesticides and persecution that did for most raptors during the 1960s and 1970s. Able to fare well in countryside or in the town, it is an adaptive and versatile bird, equally at home on cliff and mountain or urban sky-rise. The adult male has a strongly orange-brown back with dark tips to the wings and a lovely steel-grey tail. The female is generally a mottled orange-brown but again with the darker wing-tips. They can make a powerful dive, though not quite a peregrine's '*stoop*', as they drop to surprise perhaps a small bird or mammal. They will soar but follow them for long enough and they will pull up sharp and hover; always a give-away. The similarly-sized Sparrowhawk has a typical '*flap-flap-glide*' flight and tends to soar with wings splayed out much more. For the casual observer though these two do cause confusion.

Much less common though is the Merlin, that tiny predator of the high moors and the moorland fringe. They really dropped in numbers during the 1970s and 1980s and never really recovered fully. They used to pick up DDT pollution from its use on coastal farmland long after local farmers have given it up. That meant our local breeding birds that wintered on the coastal marshes collected enough DDT to stop them breeding. DDT caused their egg-shells to become very thin and so any eggs laid were crushed on the nest. In recent years they have begun to recover, but as a ground-nesting species are still very vulnerable to disturbance. A dog out of control, for example, can do enormous damage in only a few minutes on a sensitive moorland site. So it was really exciting to catch a glimpse of a male Merlin on a local moor. It was only a glimpse as it shot in a semi-stoop, rather bullet-like with wings tight in to its body, over my head. The male is a dark slate-blue on its upper parts – back, wings and tail, and has speckled white under parts. The call is similar to that of the Kestrel with a chattering *kee-kee-kee*. Kestrel is perhaps louder and higher pitched. Anyway, they can't half motor, and in a couple of seconds it had gone, passed from view. It was probably looking for a tasty Meadow Pipit or similar small bird to feed its mate or the young in the nest. For me this was an unexpected pleasure; for the Meadow Pipit unexpected but not pleasurable.

There are supposed to be quite a few Buzzards around this year, so let me know if you've seen them near you. I've also been getting some very exciting records of deer coming in. Most records have been Roe Deer, and they are definitely pushing into South Sheffield and are well established further east. There's also Muntjac around in the lowlands, and of course our Red Deer herd on the moors to the west. So do keep a look out and let me know if you see any of these three species. Please be discrete though because we still have problems of persecution and of poaching.

Exotic and alien - our changing flora and fauna

Wild Fuchsia naturalised in Cornwall. © Ian Rotherham

I'm writing this from the Lizard in Cornwall. One of the features of this exotic landscape with its mild climate and rich gardening environment is cliff-tops and hedgerows are festooned with escapees; flowers that have climbed the garden wall or leapt the garden fence. Clouds of orange *Montbretia* and the reds of naturalised *Fuchsia* enliven the area and for visitors this is part of its appeal. Tourism of course is the cornerstone of this rural economy and the swathes of exotic plants and intimate mixture of native and alien flowers *ARE* the character of Cornwall, presenting conservationists with serious dilemmas. My friend down here is James

Macfarlane, Cornwall County Council's '*invasive plants officer*' tasked with the job of controlling exotic species that damage Cornwall's environment. But where do you start? *Buddleia*, for example, is to some '*the Butterfly Bush*' but to others a nasty alien that breaks up buildings and destroys railway lines. Is it good or bad? There is no doubt that our wildlife species are changing; we are losing some and gaining others. Sometimes the gain is purely natural, for example the colonisation of Britain by the Little Egret, a beautiful diminutive white heron. In other cases the new species get here helped by people, deliberately or accidentally. This is then one of the most controversial conservation issues. It is obvious as you travel the world, that introductions of animals and plants to new areas have caused massive damage. On tropical islands in particular, they have decimated unique native species and left a legacy of a kind of '*MacDonalds ecology*' – the same everywhere you go. In North America European settlers took the '*Cockney Sparrow*' with them to remind them of home. It then became a major pest species that they tried, unsuccessfully, to eradicate.

Alien *Montbretia* lighting up a Cornish bankside. © Ian Rotherham

Closer to home the rivers, hedgerows and even some woods are increasingly dominated by a rich array of exotic and sometimes invasive species. We have the stunningly beautiful Himalayan Balsam that was spread along the River Sheaf and the River Derwent in the 1940s by Nobel Prize-winning scientist Sir Hans Krebs. It is side-by-side with the pernicious and problematic Japanese Knotweed, and the poisonous and almost vicious Giant Hogweed. Faced with these apparent threats our island wildlife seems under siege and there are campaigns to control or eradicate invasive aliens from '*natural*' habitats. In some cases these are fully justified. Japanese Knotweed, for example, causes millions of pounds damage to development sites alone, recent causalities being the new Wembley Arena and the London Olympics village. However, in many cases the situation is by no means clear-cut. The reactions to exotic species raise huge social and ethical issues as well as an array of economic and environmental ones. My friend the late Dr Oliver Gilbert was a pioneer of interest in both distinctive urban wildlife and in exotic species. His view was that change is inevitable, and we should learn to accept and even love exotic plants like Sycamore and Himalayan Balsam in our woods. This is hugely controversial, and many people shudder at the thought of the Oak-Bluebell woods becoming Sycamore-Balsam woods. However, with climate change and the impacts of urbanisation some change of this sort may be inevitable. Ollie was also the champion of Japanese Knotweed along the urban rivers. His pioneering research undertaken in Sheffield during the 1980s led to the suggestion that these were distinctive and appropriate urban communities to celebrate and foster. Excitingly he found an '*ancient woodland flora*' (Bluebell, Wood Anemone, and Woodrush) establishing under the dense stands of Knotweed all the way along the urban Rivers Sheaf and Don. These areas also became home to good numbers of the now threatened native Water Vole, but then predated by alien Mink. However, Ollie didn't live to see the return of the Rover Don Otters now lying up under the superb cover of... (you guessed it), Japanese Knotweed. When his findings were announced at a major conference of the British Ecological Society, in many quarters of the conservation movement they went down like the proverbial lead budgie!

Himalayan Balsam. © Ian Rotherham

Oh Deer Not Again!

Surprising for many local people, there could well be a wild deer on your doorstep, or at least at the end of the garden. Even twenty years ago this would have been unthinkable. But now you have a pretty good chance of either of our two smaller species: the native Roe, and the alien Muntjac. In a few areas, but increasingly you might see Red Deer too. Fallow Deer, introduced to deer parks by the Normans, is restricted to a few areas and mostly pop up around the Dukeries, where some are white forms. This is a bit of a shock if sighted after an evening visit to the local pub and has led to hardened drinkers fore-swearing the demon alcohol! However, going west towards Stanton and Matlock in the Peak there is a chance of another unusual sight, that of a black or melanistic herd of Fallow Deer. As with several local herds, these can be traced back to their medieval ancestors.

Back in the 1990s, I co-ordinated the first regional survey of deer populations. The first wild records, which began in the 1980s, included animals from the feral herd of Red Deer at Wharncliffe Wood which now began to be seen right in the heart of industrial Sheffield having followed the River Don down into the Kelham island area. Inspection of the islands in the River Don suggested that they were quite regular visitors down there. As Sheffield City Council's ecologist, I was out and about meeting and working with farmers and foresters and others. They began to pass on records of what were clearly Roe Deer, our smaller native species. When we first reported these sightings they were generally dismissed with a comment of there are no wild deer in our region other than the feral Red herd. However, with friends and colleagues, Andy McCarthy, Peter Wolstenholme and Richard Wilson (from the regional branch of the British Deer Society), and especially Colin Howes of Doncaster Museum, we generated over 1,000 new records and sightings of deer across the region. We actually began in Sheffield, where local experts told us there were no deer, or at least very few, but within a few weeks the area of search expanded to take in Barnsley, Rotherham, and Doncaster. Northwards we stretched to Leeds and Bradford, southwards to Nottingham, and in the west we covered the whole of the Peak District. The results were outstanding and re-wrote the picture of deer in this region. Excitingly for an ecologist, we captured the early stages of colonisation into the area, and especially the movement of deer into the conurbations. Work quickly involved the press, the radio, and even TV. The research was covered by regional television, and then picked up in a big way by Radio 4. Coverage by *The Star* and BBC Radio Sheffield helped involve hundreds of volunteer recorders across the area. After a year or so the study was also noticed by researchers nationally, and the reports and papers were presented at major conferences. We then became known as the centre for work on both urban deer nationally, and especially for deer seen in and from, people's gardens.

Since then the work has continued but in a more low-key way. However, records have kept coming in, and the deer have kept spreading. With a bit of luck now, if you are out and about on the Peak District moors you have a good chance of seeing a herd of Red Deer. Considering that this is really the first time since the great medieval deer parks and hunting chases that you might see this, it really is a privilege. As our largest land mammal, a Red Deer stag, especially in rut, is pretty awesome.

Red Deer stag bellowing. © Paul Hobson

Not everyone agrees though, and some are not happy to see deer in the area. I accept that they can be a problem. This is especially so if deer come into your garden and eat your prize rose-bushes, for example. There is also a worry about deer ticks and the spread of diseases such as Lyme Disease and so there is the need to take sensible precautions. However, these problems can be avoided or overcome pretty easily, so overall it should be a big welcome for the return of the natives.

There are a few issues around Muntjac as they spread around Britain (often illegally assisted in the back of a transit van), from areas in the south to which they were introduced. For a start they are not native to Britain, but also they can have a devastating impact on woodlands by eating Bluebells and other wild flowers. Both Muntjac and Roe can be heard barking at night around the urban fringes of Sheffield, Rotherham, Doncaster and Sheffield. Their rather wheezy hoarse bark can carry half a mile or more, and is produced late evening and into the early hours, often around December, April and August. We've had recent records all the way into Meersbrook in Sheffield. So look out, there's a deer about!

More Deer Records please!

Our regional deer survey continues and some really exciting records coming in. Only a couple of weeks ago Fraser Ludlam sent in a sighting from the Barlow area of Derbyshire, and really very interesting! He saw two Roe Deer around about midnight and the next day his friend reported two in a field close by. We've not had many records of Roe from that area, so it is a very useful record. We've also had reports of Roe Deer around Rivelin Valley, but I need these to be confirmed. Has anybody else seen them? We're still receiving information on sightings of Red Deer across the region, and Muntjac too. Some of the latter are getting quite urban; so do keep a look out and let us know. My colleague Martin Derbyshire will be very pleased to hear from you as he is busy writing up his Masters dissertation and compiling one of Britain's biggest interactive computer databases on deer populations; all with your help!! Just as a reminder we are interested in all records of deer across the region, and not just new ones.

Commonplace but special

I recently had chance to meet one of my favourite environmental writers, a lady called Sue Clifford, from an organisation called *Common Ground*. The title of her first well-known book back in the 1980s was '*Holding Your Ground*', and we got an honourable mention for the sterling work of the Moss Valley Wildlife Group in defeating Sheffield City Council at the Green Belt Public Enquiry. This was an almost unprecedented set-back for a major local authority. The area in question in the lower Moss Valley remains open countryside as a consequence of work by our first local wildlife group. But back to Sue; she and the organisation *Common Ground*, have spent many years promoting the idea of local character and local distinctiveness for people and conservation. This is a message that has finally got through to agencies and others; largely, I think, due to Sue's writing and indeed her enthusiasm. If any of you have been to '*Apple Days*' or '*Orchard Days*', to savour, celebrate and hopefully safeguard now rare English varieties of apples, then these are the people who originally thought up the idea. Her latest book with Angela King '*England in Particular – A celebration of the commonplace,*

the local, the vernacular and the distinctive' is a delight to read and if anyone is planning ahead, it would make an ideal stocking-filler for Christmas! It really is the sort of book that anybody interested in the countryside, in the environment, or in local history would be fascinated by. Much of what Sue campaigns and writes about is the importance of the everyday and the ordinary. This is pretty much the sort of thing I write about for *The Star*. One of our problems in conservation is that we often don't think something is worth bothering about until it becomes rare, and by then it is often too late anyway.

Are domestic apples a threatened resource? © Ian Rotherham

Whilst talking to Sue, I was standing in the car park of the grounds of a local college, one-time mental asylum, and former grand house, with a lovely wooded landscape. This was the day after we had a torrential downpour and floods across northern parts of our region. But today the sun was shining, there was a late-summer glow in the air, and I suddenly noticed how Robins were singing through all the woods and the wooded gardens. It seemed especially noticeable because for a couple of months there's been almost no bird-song. I wonder if you noticed this too – the sudden starting up of the autumn and winter chorus of Robins. This is a part of Sue Clifford's ordinary landscape, and what makes the everyday and commonplace special for each one of us. Of course the Robin is one of the only native song-birds to sing throughout the year, and this is largely because it establishes and defends a winter territory as well as a summer one. Its song is not to entertain us, but to warn off other Robins. It's what makes our local patch important to every one of us. So, like the Kingfisher that John Parr emailed me about on one of the streams above Totley, it is nice to see and special for us when we do. John's Kingfisher was the first he'd seen there for many years, and I suspect was a non-breeding bird moving around looking for suitable habitat. With local rivers now generally much cleaner than they used to be, and the series of generally short, mild winters we've had, Kingfishers are doing well. Of course Sheffield is famous for its urban and industrial Kingfishers along the Don, Sheaf, Porter and the rest. When these birds or, for example, our riverside Grey Herons, appear to an urban audience they generally have a big impact. You can stand in Sheffield City Centre and have a reasonable chance of a Grey Heron drifting lazily overhead like some prehistoric Pterodactyl. Nature is coming to town.

Red Kites and Reintroductions – the case of the missing Lynx

European Lynx. © Ian Rotherham

Sheila Johnson from Woodseats emailed me after my column about Red Kite reintroductions. This was partly to say she enjoyed the article and how wonderful the Red Kite is, but also to ask a very interesting and pertinent question about the issues, ethics and guidelines for reintroductions. The question was basically what can we or should we reintroduce and why? Also there is the issue of what is legal and what guidelines help us decide what is appropriate. Sheila asks: '*There are I suppose species lost through the*

natural progression of things and a great many others through human intervention. Shouldn't species that are lost to an area through a natural process remain lost? (I know no one's thinking of reintroducing T-Rex). And should only species sacrificed to human habitation be considered ethical for reintroduction.' Well Sheila, many thanks for your email, but wow, this is a really big issue. It is an interesting and tricky question with lots to consider, though I can't go into much detail here. There are strict guidelines drawn up for the UK by Defra and the UK Government agencies. I must say that some of the issues and guidance are questionable, and there are serious matters of ethics to consider. This even applies to what we classify as '*alien*' or '*exotic*' (and why), and what is, or was '*native*', and so might be considered fit for reintroduction. There is also a question of what can or should be introduced or reintroduced. It is fair to say that we are not totally consistent in terms of what we consider ok or desirable. You would think that it is straightforward, but it really isn't. So for example, one of our local mammals in Sheffield and the Peak District is the Mountain Hare, a Local Red Data Book species. It *is* native to Britain but was introduced to our region as a game animal. It is a bit of a star and so we like it as a kind of honorary native. For bird-watchers, of course, we now accept the Little Owl as an honorary native but I still remember older local naturalists around Bradfield, for example, calling it the '*Frenchie*', introduced from France. There was even a campaign by land-owners in the 1930s to eradicate what they saw as a pest and decimator of game birds; all totally unfounded of course. There was a wonderful but fortunately short-lived Victorian body called the *Acclimatisation Society* that wanted to introduce all sorts of birds and mammals to Britain: Buffaloes, Wallabies and many more! Along with the Victorian wild gardeners, these people were responsible for many and varied introductions of wildlife to Britain. Most failed, but a fair number have survived and thrived.

The question then is what we do about reintroducing animals, birds or maybe plants that have become extinct. Again it is not as simple as it at first sounds. Why did they disappear and to what extent was it through human agency? If people caused extinction then are the conditions now suited to reintroduction? What will the impacts of reintroduction be? And often not asked, what are the consequences of not doing so? Species like Beaver and Wild Boar, for example, are hugely important in 'natural' woodlands, so without them the ecology is changed. Suggest bringing them back, however, and a lot of people will be very concerned. Yet the Wild Boar is already now re-established from escapes from Boar farms, but Defra doesn't know whether to treat them as native or alien. For deliberate reintroductions there is also a scientific argument that we hear less often now; that it is better to allow nature to take its course. This, of course, doesn't always happen and a helping hand may be needed, like the Red Kites. For the Cornish Choughs this wasn't so. With conservation bodies ready for reintroductions, wild birds from Brittany arrived and established independently. Nice one and 'one nil' to nature!

In July 2006, I was one of thirty researchers invited from North America and Europe for a transatlantic Workshop held in Zurich; the theme was 're-wilding'. This included exciting topics like the reintroduction of large grazing herbivores and carnivores to parts of Europe and North America from where they became extinct. There are serious arguments for introducing the African Elephant to North America in place of lost Mammoths and Mastodons from 11,000 years ago. Not *T. Rex* yet, but getting there! I think it is now highly likely, for example, that the European Lynx will eventually be reintroduced to parts of the Scottish Highlands to help control the deer populations. Now wouldn't that be exciting?

Of Dragons and Damsels

Southern Hawker Dragonfly. © Mr & Mrs East

Patricia Brown sent some lovely close-up pictures of a large dragonfly in her garden. It is a female or possibly a young male of the species I wrote about recently, the Brown Hawker or *Aeshna grandis*. I'm not sure where her garden is, but this is a dragon to watch out for. About the same time, I had a message from Janice East of Sheffield, with some wonderful pictures taken by her husband in their garden. She said: '*My Mum cut out your article from Saturday's* Star. *This picture was taken 27th June, in our garden in Ketton Avenue. We've had our pond about four years and have always had plenty of wildlife and frogs but this year, around June, there were dragonflies every day. We had lots of tadpoles which 'disappeared' and one day there were at least ten dragonflies 'drying off' on reeds around the pond. It was a shame that at the time it was raining so much, I didn't know if this would affect them or not. I've read your article about golden ringed dragonflies, ours seem to be about 3 or 4 inches long and wingspan, but we have no idea what sort they are, I'd appreciate it if you could let me know, I've been looking on the internet but am none the wiser.*'

Southern Hawker Dragonfly emerging. © Mr & Mrs East

Well it is quite difficult to identify dragonflies as superficially they do look very similar. These pictures show one of our larger dragons – the Southern Hawker or *Aeshna cyanea*, and yes, this may be where the tadpoles went – but then dragonflies do have to eat!! One of the difficulties in identifying them is that there are several closely-related species that all look pretty much the same. The males and females are marked differently, and those photographed by Janice's husband had just emerged. They are drying out with wings along the back rather than stuck out sideways in the usual dragonfly pose. At this stage the colours and markings are also rather washed out – until they dry and gain their full adult markings. Janice was also interested in the bees I mentioned in the summer, and would love to keep bees. Perhaps any beekeepers out there might write in to say how you go about setting up. I'd be interested to know. Something else Janice mentioned was the overgrown garden that used to be close to where she lives, and the other green spaces around there. It forms a fantastic little wildlife haven with loads of birds and mammals like Foxes. It is so important in your wildlife garden to have a bit of untidiness to let the animals and wild flowers in. But the other vital ingredient is keeping a bit of '*spare*' land, or what we used to call '*waste*' land nearby. These are the little green spaces that seem uncared for and unkempt, but which keep the urban ecosystem ticking over. The danger is that whilst most of us appreciate the wildlife when we see it, these sites are taken for granted and easily lost. In many parts of the region you've a good chance of seeing fox, even in broad daylight; often they lie up and even breed in old Bramble beds and the like. In some areas you'll also, if you are very lucky, have a chance of Badger as well. It really is a veritable jungle out there.

As we move inexorably towards autumn, the big dragonflies come into their own, with individuals appearing all over the place. I had a beautiful Southern Hawker, all greens and blues, swooping through my wildlife garden this week. However, there is one species to look for and easy to identify, the Brown Hawker. It is big, and will be coming to a garden near you. This will turn up almost anywhere. I recall a particularly quiet moment at Bramall Lane a few years ago, when one was hawking over the kop. It caused quite a stir. In fact, I seem to remember it was the most excitement we had all afternoon! It has a long brown body, and the shimmering wings have a distinctive golden yellow sheen. Another interesting thing with big dragonflies in particular, is there territorial behaviour and their way of hunting. They are really active predators and stalk their patch in search of prey. I watched a Southern Hawker in Graves Park the other day, patrolling up and down a line of trees just by

Norton Woodseats Cricket Club. They spend a lot of time on the wing (which uses a lot of energy), and so they also find a suitable perch on which to land, and to survey the landscape, possible rivals, mates, and of course, food. They move between good hunting areas and breeding sites, usually rivers or ponds, depending on the species. Here again they are both territorial and aggressive. Males chase off rivals and await females with whom to mate. The females will return later to lay their eggs, and so the whole cycle begins again. Just imagine what the prehistoric dragonflies were like with a wingspan of about eighteen inches – a serious dragonfly! Now the really spectacular dragon for us, and we are really very lucky to have them close by, is the Golden Ringed Dragonfly. This is an insect of the upland, the moors and bogs. It breeds in and around upland streams, and frequents the surrounding moorland and bog habitat. It is a good 2-3 inches long (6-7cms) and has a rich, jet-black body with yellow-golden rings around its abdomen (the long part of the body). They are quite rare nationally but we have a good population in the Peak District. If you want to see one, then generally you will need to go up into the hills to find them.

Golden Ringed Dragonfly on the author's arm. © Ian Rotherham

Questions I have been asked

How do spiders hear? Well, surprisingly, it is by means of their hairy legs and this is why they are so hairy!

This isn't a dragonfly that moves away from its favoured habitat, so you want a warm, still day and head up to Stanage Edge and Ringinglow Bog near Redmires, or up onto White Edge near Froggatt. You can then find a quiet spot near a bit of bog or perhaps a stream, and sit and wait. The other strategy is to roam around suitable areas and just keep a look-out. If they are about you will see them, and they are pretty obvious!

Questions that I have been asked

How long do spiders live? This varies but for most British species it would be somewhere between about six and twelve months which includes the egg stage. House Spiders seem to live longer and grow faster in hot humid summers and some can get to be real monsters. Tropical Tarantulas can live up to twenty years.

Garden Spider. © Mr & Mrs East

Magic Mushrooms and that autumnal feeling

You can tell it is autumn, partly as the days shorten and the nights grow longer, but especially as the '*magic mushroom*' pickers descend on acidic grasslands and moors around Sheffield and Barnsley. This little mushroom (*Psilocybe semilanceata* or Liberty Cap) is relatively common on slightly acidic lawns, grasslands, and roadsides, and now attracts a wide interest with mystique accorded to its hallucinogenic properties. The eagle-eye of the law also now

takes an interest in the possession of mushroom-based products too! Here in Britain we are deeply distrustful of all manner of fungi except for the good old Field Mushroom. Indeed we generally take comfort in often inferior products from a supermarket, with possible chemical additives, rather than the diversity of wild mushroom available. A sensible reason underlies this approach today in that we as a community mostly can't identify the safe ones, and the nasty ones can be exceedingly nasty. I have personal experience of this because as a very small child I accidentally, or at least unknowingly, ate some probably totally benign '*mushrooms*' in our back garden. However, the consequences were severe as adults rushed me to A&E at the local hospital. Here I was give a forcible stomach pump, and I can tell you it was not a nice experience; certainly not for a three-year old. Basically, if in doubt then leave well alone. In some ways it is a shame since if you travel into Europe there is a much stronger tradition of culinary fungi. Even here it is now possible to buy a reasonable diversity of commercially-grown fungi such as Oyster Mushrooms, and Chinese Shiitake.

A good deal of the emerging interest in mushrooms and other fungi over recent years has been promoted by experts and enthusiasts from Sheffield, such as Patrick Harding, Tony Lyons and others. Along with this there is a new interest in wild foods and cooking based on natural products. Autumn is then the prime time for the new mushroom enthusiasts to emerge and scour the landscape in search of rich pickings. If you are interested in joining them then check out your local natural history society, wildlife group, or National Trust site such as Longshaw or Clumber Park, as they will most likely be holding guided events, especially for beginners. However, the wider roles of fungi, not just those whose fruits we pick and eat, are also fascinating. These are the organisms – not animals or plants, but a separate Kingdom of the Fungi that power many ecosystems. They support the great trees such as Oaks and Beeches, whose roots are sheathed by fungal growths vital to nutrient uptake. Semi-natural grasslands have networks of fungi underground, connecting the grasses and herbs in a complex web of plant, soil and fungus. Even the heaths and moors are driven by myriad unseen microscopic fungi in the roots of Heather and Bilberry. Many food and drink processes are products of fungal activities; the most obvious being yeasts for baking and brewing. There are many other uses too, not least the medical applications of antibiotics such as Penicillin, originally from a fungus.

It isn't all good of course, Nature never is. Fungi can be destructive and cause diseases, for us and for our garden plants, and pets. Look at your Rose bushes and you'll see the tell-tale black spots of a fungal infection; which, if given chance will wreak havoc. At this time of year especially there is a very similar Tar Spot disease of Sycamore Trees. Take a look at the leaves on a Sycamore Tree near where you live and it will be covered by brownish-black spots. These don't seem to actually cause too much harm to the tree and Sycamores are known for their fast growth. There is another twist too. Black Spot on Roses and Tar Spot on Sycamores both tell us about air quality. Those of you who grew up when our region was one of the worst polluted in the World, may recall the absence of these diseases from most parts of the area. It would be interesting if anyone can remember when they first noticed the black spots on either Roses or Sycamores. I can still recall going to Lancaster University in the 1970s and puzzling over Sycamore leaves covered in Tar Spot. I'd never seen anything like this at home in Sheffield. At Lancaster, close to the west coast and the clean Atlantic air, the lack of sulphur pollution allowed the fungus to grow and the Sycamores and Roses to suffer. Swings and roundabouts I suppose.

Anybody seen a Parrot recently?

It isn't every day that you see a Parrot in our region; at least not yet anyway. I remember as a child my Uncle Ken on Warminster Road in Sheffield seeing what he thought was a green Parrot in the trees at the bottom of his garden. Eventually, and helped by the *Observer's Book of Birds*, we worked out that it was actually a Green Woodpecker; by no means common at that time or in that area. As a ten-year old I was duly excited and impressed! An unexpected sighting of Waxwings on a Cotoneaster bush a couple of years later also conjured up ideas of Parrots too, but once again the *Observer's Book of Birds* helped with a correct identification. Despite

these early failures to actually see a real Parrot in Sheffield, when I went to King Edwards School on Glossop Road there was a moderate success. The old Botanical Gardens boasted two Macaws, along with a very impressive Piranha in the adjacent aquarium. These were clearly the stars of the show and very popular with local people. And at last there was a chance to see a 'wild' or at least free-flying Parrot – when the Macaws went on an avian 'walkabout' and spent several days perched on a roof-top of a house on Brocco Bank. Now here are a couple of questions that some *Star* readers might be able to answer. Firstly, does anybody remember the names and colours of the two Parrots? I know one was very tame and the other seriously bad-tempered; and it is best to keep well away from a bad-tempered Macaw. My other question is whether only one of the Macaws or both escaped? I remember freedom was short-lived and they were back on the perches within a week or so. I wonder what became of them when the aviary finally closed down.

The Sheffield Botanical Gardens Macaw. © Paula Smithers

A couple of years ago, Paul Ardron and I saw a Cockatiel at Chatsworth, and I must say it did look rather out of place. However, even that pales into normality by comparison with a blue Budgerigar flying over the old Waverley opencast coal site back in the 1980s. That really did have an '*other worldly*' feel to it. Now it might surprise you to know that it may not be too long before seeing a Parrot in the region may become commonplace. In London the Ring-necked Parakeet is now well-established, with flocks of these spectacular birds roaming the suburbs. This species originates from either Africa or India, depending on the sub-species.

They eat fruit, berries and seeds, and nest in tree-holes. Moving around in large, colourful flocks they have become an exciting and generally popular addition to urban birdlife. It seems that as a long-standing escape as a cage-bird in Britain from at least the 1830s, wild flocks have been established around London since the 1930s. They have also bred in northern England, including in Manchester since the 1970s. We do get records of Parakeets in our area, and one of the most recent was from Jan Turner of the Gleadless Valley Wildlife Trust, in Meersbrook. In recent weeks a single bird has been seen feeding in local gardens, and I wonder how long it will be before we get a regular breeding population. There are a few records in the Sheffield Bird Study Group annual reports, but not that many. Has anybody else seen this or other birds locally? Of course, as an 'alien' species I wonder whether there will be calls for control and eradication. If anyone from the RSPB reads this, then please do let me know what the official policy is.

More on the Parrots

The article a couple of weeks ago has certainly stirred up a few memories and also some very recent records. We've also been able to piece together some of the history of the two Macaws at Sheffield's Botanical Gardens. So Mavis Gosney of Ringinglow Road recalls that the two birds were stolen (with a value she thinks) of around £1,000 each. Mavis also believes that this was why the aviary was closed. However, she couldn't remember their names, so other correspondents have come to the rescue. Verena Bishop of Sheffield 6 says they were called Jack and Poppet; the larger was a red Macaw and the smaller a blue and yellow one.

The Sheffield Botanical Gardens Macaw. © Paula

Smithers

Apparently they would both sit on her arm, the blue and yellow Macaw systematically stripping the toggles off Verena's duffle coat. But we do have a slight disagreement here as P. Settle-Bamber thinks they were named Popit and Charlie, and that Popit was stolen from the Gardens in the early 1980s. Pete has also e-mailed in to say that at least one, but maybe both birds were stolen one night and never found. Paula Smithers sent in a lovely photograph of two nursing friends in 1972 posing with the blue and yellow Macaw. She says that they were at the School of Nursing just off Clarkehouse Road, and used to walk around the Gardens in their lunchtimes. They loved the aquarium, and of course the aviary. Now John Highfield at *The Star* tells me that the parrots were used in the making of a classic (i.e. early) film version of Treasure Island, and sort of retired to Sheffield. This sounds a bit dodgy but could be true. Surely somebody knows the complete story – what were their names (we now have Charlie, Popit or Poppet, and Jack), when did they escape to Hunter's Bar, and when were they stolen? Also were they really stars of stage and screen? Do any of the Friends of the Botanical Gardens know, or perhaps my old friend Arroll Winning?

I must say that I was also rather moved by Verena's story of her family's green Amazonian Parrot that had to be re-housed when her family lost their home during the Blitz. Polly the Parrot (I jest not) was only saved from being crushed when the bomb hit by the strength of her large cage – one lucky parrot. She ended up with the caretaker at Pyebank School during 1940, but was reunited with her original family after the war ended. So it was a happy ending for Polly, Verena and family. Since parrots are both long-lived and highly intelligent, I do know that they form very close attachments to individuals and to families. My neighbours at Charnock a few years ago, Eddie and Sheila, had an African Grey Parrot that did the most wonderful impressions of people's voices. This was even to the extent that it would '*speak*' at the right point in a conversation – '*Tara then*' and '*See yeh*' – as you were leaving. You had to be very careful what you said in front of it. I wonder if anybody remembers the two Mynah Birds at Godley Gardens on Abbeydale Road, back in the 1970s. The lads that I worked with in the Garden Centre taught them to swear at the good people of Dore and Totley. That kept us amused – happy days!

One of the famous parrots photographed in the 1960s. © Jim Buckley

Anyway we've also had more reports of Parakeets in the region. Jan Turner has not seen the Meersbrook bird for a few weeks, but *The Star's* own Paul License had one fly past his dining room window in southeast Sheffield. He's heard them calling since then. Probably the same birds were seen in Woodhouse by David Newbould. He describes one as mostly grey with yellow cheeks, and the other bright green. They were making their usual characteristic shrieks and squawks. The birds were being mobbed by Magpies, which unfortunately is often the case. I wonder if these include the same bird that was seen in Meersbrook, or is there really a bit of an influx to the region. Please keep a look out and let me know. Has anyone over in Rotherham, Barnsley, or Doncaster seen any, now or in the past?

Winter Visitors and Autumn Migrants

I've had a few letters and emails about local sightings. N. Hobson from Millhouses wrote in about Kingfishers after I mentioned John Parr's record near Totley. Apparently he has seen them on the River Sheaf during 2005. Excitingly this was the first time since 1975 or 1976! That was back in my early days as a keen birdwatcher too, and I think he and I saw the same birds. They used to nest on the River and in summer would fly up and down to catch small fish for their nestlings. Some of the house-holders near Abbey Lane used to get them right outside their back windows. It really is great to know that they are back.

I've also had a note from Mark and Sally at the Grouse Inn at Froggatt to say how much they and their regulars enjoy the Red Deer that have moved into the area in recent years. So far I have had quite a few new records come in and everyone is pleased to see or hear the Deer. In fact a number of people have commented on the noise of the Red Deer rutting at the moment. It is one of our wildlife spectacles and very impressive when heard for the first time. It is a loud roaring made by the stags as they work themselves up into a frenzy. This is generally in the late evening but sometimes during the day. One correspondent has asked whether the stags are dangerous, and the answer is potentially yes, but really very unlikely. Most accidents are with stags in captivity at close quarters. Obviously though, it is best to give a large animal like a Red Deer plenty of respect, and that means space between you and it. Anyway keep the records coming in. I would expect those of you over towards Doncaster might see a few Red Deer too, and you also have an excellent chance of either or both Roe Deer and Muntjac.

This time of year is all change for nature. Wild flowers are dying back for the winter, the summer birds have mostly left, and the autumn migration is well underway. All across Europe waves of birds are moving south. In some places the movements provide spectacular views and experiences for birdwatchers that also '*flock*' to key locations to see one of nature's great events. However, migration is something that occurs on our doorstep too. It also occurs for different species during daylight hours and for many birds at night too. If you stand outside on a quiet evening and listen carefully you'll almost certainly hear the soft calls of migrating thrushes. Many of these will be Redwings, a small cousin of the Song Thrush, flying south from the arctic and tundra lands that are their summer breeding areas. What may be more noticeable too are flocks of wild Geese. Now you have to be careful with your identification. Many of the sightings these days are Canada Geese, widely established and increasing across the region. They call loudly and fly noisily, often quite low and late into the dusk. I had around fifteen pass at rooftop level over my garden in Norton just the other day. They may be alien species but they do add a feeling of real wildlife to the suburbs! Now the other Geese to look out for in our area are usually Pink-footed Geese. These are migrant birds that breed way up in the north, and are presently moving from great wetlands in north-western Britain, across the country to the Wash and the Cambridgeshire and Lincolnshire Fens. Now get a map out and look what that means. They fly almost straight over our region, although generally in v-formation or in long, straggly lines, and at high altitude. Worth watching for, but don't be fooled by lines of gulls, or of course smaller wildfowl such as ducks. As always, do let me know if you see any of these, but also please do send your records in to the local bird recorders.

Canada Goose. © Ian Rotherham

It's all a Bit Fishy

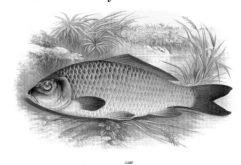

Carp. From a Victorian print

Saturday's *Star* (November 11th) raised an interesting issue and one that I want to follow up. Both the article on page 11 (*River patrols stepped up over fish row*) and the *Star Opinion* (*Fishy problem must be tackled*) were highlighting the issue of coarse fish in local rivers being '*illegally*' caught for food, mostly it seems, by recent immigrants from Eastern Europe. The article noted that '*Eating coarse fish such as tench, bream and perch is common in many countries, particularly in Eastern Europe, but it is frowned upon in Britain*'. Now this does present some interesting issues. I have to say that I'm not a fisherman and I've always struggled with the concept of catching the fish and throwing them back. However, I do respect the sportsmen and women that indulge in this. I can see the point a little more, of the fly fishermen catching salmon and trout for the pot, or similarly sea anglers catching mackerel, *etc*. But sports fishery and competitive angling are huge recreational activities across our region and I can respect that and admire the skill and patience required.

However, what does interest me is our attitude towards what we eat and what we don't. There's also an assumption by many people that we would never eat say, carp, and never have. Of course this is baloney. Hugh Fearnley-Whittingstall in '*A Cook on the Wild Side*' notes that '*...much of the angling fraternity in this country take a pretty dim view of anybody killing and eating their beloved coarse fish.*' Apparently Hugh's programme where he cooked and ate a small Carp he'd caught in the Thames attracted a mass of hostile letters and articles in the angling press. So it is clear that this is a tricky topic and that passions run deep. Yet, as Hugh points out, a major reason why we have so many ponds and so many Carp, certainly historically, in Britain is because it was such a good food. Indeed it was one of the staple foods for most people. Especially on a Friday when meat-eating was prohibited on religious grounds, Carp from the fish pond was a mainstay. This was indulged in by monks and other religious groups, but was also promoted actively by the church to its people. One major reason was pure economics. The monasteries often held a monopoly over the supply of fish for food, and so made a lot of money by insisting on religious observance and supplying the alternative – at a price! We have benefited with a legacy of historic fish ponds across the region, such as at Beauchief Abbey for example. But don't forget that these were not for pleasure but for the table or to make money.

For medieval communities fish was almost as vital as bread. The Catholic Church laid down rules that on Fridays, (and at one time, Saturdays and Wednesdays too) meat was forbidden. For the period of Lent too, eggs and other dairy products were also forbidden. In effect this meant that for about half the days of the year, everyone had to eat vegetables or other foods, either alone or with fish. Clergymen themselves had even more strictly applied rules for what foods were allowed. There were some slightly bizarre consequences of these restrictions. One was that some animals were kind of honorary fish and were allowed. So Puffins and Barnacle Geese were okay because they were believed to be '*created at sea*'. Similarly, if you were near the coast you could eat seals, and the so-called '*Royal Fish*' – the whale, Sturgeon, and Porpoise. Although for these you'd need the King's permission. Oh, and Beaver was acceptable too, as it supposedly had a fish's tail!

I'd love to hear from you about this and your views on the whole issue. Has anyone tried Carp or say Pike? How about those with family from Eastern Europe? Have you or do you eat traditional carp for example? And a question for the older people; does anybody remember '*Perchines*' during the 1940s? Let me know in the next couple of weeks and we'll come back to this!

Perch. From a Victorian print

Carp and chips

In Domesday South Yorkshire (then the West Riding) say around 1100 AD, fisheries or *piscariae* were recorded along the major rivers and streams, including Barnby-upon-Don. Also over past Doncaster were twenty fish ponds supposedly at Tudworth, but possibly these were spread across the wider land-holdings of William De Warenne, the Lord of Conisbrough Manor. These ponds generated around 20,000 eels per year; a pretty impressive haul. However, if you cast an eye over maps of the region you will pick out numbers of fish ponds around ancient sites of manor houses and monasteries. As I said a couple of weeks ago, fish and especially coarse fish, were a staple part of the diet for our medieval ancestors, and remain so today in many parts of the world. The ponds we have inherited today are a wonderful wildlife and recreational resource, and of course totally irreplaceable.

In England and Wales coarse fish as a food came to a resounding halt when, in about 1539-40, King Henry VIII abolished the monasteries, having severed ties with the Roman Catholic Church through the *Act of Supremacy* in 1534. Through this he removed many of the constraints and protocols surrounding the daily diets of the English. This move also broke the monopoly that had been held in many areas by the monasteries to supply fish commercially. At the same time, with naval fleets and transport increasing, there was an increased use of sea fish or white fish. These had previously been expensive and so were only the food of the wealthy or of communities very close to the coast. As an island race the English took to sea fish like the proverbial '*duck to water*', and the carp was consigned to a culinary backwater. In the largely land-locked and often Catholic countries of Eastern Europe this clearly was not the case. So my friends in the Czech Republic will dine this Christmas on a '*Christmas Carp*', rather than a Turkey. Whilst visiting Poland and the Ukraine over the last two years I have also had chance to try the local Carp. And the verdict …in Poland the fish served were very small and incredibly bony, more Minnow than Carp, but in Ukraine we were served absolute monsters freshly barbecued and straight out of the Forest University's own Carp pond; and they were delicious. The copious beer and vodka helped enormously too.

A Pike

However, I've had an email from a reader to say how much he enjoyed the article on fish and fish-ponds, but also to give the angler's viewpoint. This was basically that in the UK we tend to fish for coarse fish such as Carp as competition angling. The joy is in the catch of a big fish, which is then returned to the river or lake to get even bigger. If the catch is taken for 'the pot' then of course this doesn't happen. Also of course, in more recent time the eating of most coarse fish has not been a custom in the UK. There was more though, and this answers a query I had about Pike. I was always told it was a very earthy fish to eat, but also that it was good and a bit like Trout. Well apparently it depends on the

water. In clean, fast-flowing water it is good to eat, but in slow-flowing or muddy waters it is rather earthy and not desperately pleasant. So there you are, and you read it here first! The same person also wrote in with a useful lead from a correspondent on the '*Perchines*' that I asked about. There's an excellent web site with all sorts of interesting information, but more on that another time.

I had a really interesting letter from J.P. Russell of Sheffield 8 in response to my question about Pike. The family used to go fishing in the 1960s and would sometimes catch Pike along with the other coarse fish. Usually the Pike ended up being taken back as cat-food. However, a neighbour apparently offered to cook one; and with a recipe that sounds like one I've used for Trout (butter, herbs, wrapped in foil and oven-baked). Anyway the result and verdict … delicious!!

On the track of the Variegated Yellow Archangel coming to a wood near you very soon!

I wrote before about alien, exotic species invading our region. I've also raised issues about our reactions, and that it isn't always as clear cut as you'd think. Well I'd like your help in tracking one of these newcomers to the area, and remarkably it is new to science too. This is a very special plant, the cousin of the native Yellow Archangel of ancient woodlands, or *Lamium galeobdolon*, if you want to be clever. The latter is known as Yellow Deadnettle, and along with favourites such as Bluebell, is a plant of old woods, copses and ancient hedgerows.

The Variegated Archangel has doubled its chromosomes and become more vigorous. It is a very interesting plant with a rather mysterious history; not formally known to science until the early 1960s when it was recorded by botanists in Central and Eastern Europe. However, now with help from gardeners and gardening experts we have delved more deeply into its background and traced it as a prized garden cultivar in collections from the 1930s and 1940s; but we think back to the Victorians. Many of you gardeners will know that the Victorians loved variegated plants; they established major collections of them and produced new and varied types. Now for the purist, the variegated Yellow Archangel isn't actually 'variegated' as such – the white blotches are caused by air pockets or vacuoles in the leaves; but that's for the expert gardeners to debate. For us it is spectacularly variegated and that is one reason why people like it. It also produces stunning heads of bright yellow flowers like mini Snap-Dragons; supposedly like an angel with its wings spread, and hence the name.

Variegated Yellow Archangel. © Ian Rotherham

Variegated Yellow Archangel. © Ian Rotherham

A few years ago one of my students (Charlotte Cousins) at Sheffield Hallam University did a survey of the wild plant in our area, and collected case-studies of its escape or introduction by local gardeners. It doesn't set seeds and its spread is totally through people introducing it. This was all with help from the local media, especially *The Star*, and now's your chance to get involved and help again. I want information on sites across the region with wild Variegated Yellow Archangel; and if you have deliberately or accidentally helped its '*escape*' then I would like to hear from you! One of my students, Melissa May carried out a further study and I am interested in how Variegated Archangel outgrows its native competitors. It seems to begin to grow much earlier in the year than the native plant – perhaps the key to its success, producing stunning shoots of green/silver/white leaves in dense, abundant clusters. Look at the plant now and you will see what I mean, especially where there is plenty of light – such as the edge of a wood, or in a hedgerow. Here it forms dense, almost impenetrable patches that appear to swamp out native woodland flowers. Is this enough to make the plant such a success? What we don't yet know is whether it is able to penetrate deep into ancient woodland; in shadier conditions its competitive nature seems to reduce to about that of the native.

Anyway we need to know when the Variegated Archangel first comes into flower; and we need your help. Even if it is in your garden, I need to know when you first spot the yellow flowers of the Archangel emerging and it can be early in the year. In 2007, I gave a prize of a book on ancient woodlands by Sheffield '*History Man*', Hallam University's own Professor Melvyn Jones, and the recent publication by Julie Bunting on '*Bygone Industries of the Peak*' to those sending records in. I'm still looking forward to more records of early-flowering Archangel.

The seasons are marked by patterns of flowers and by the comings and goings of birds. Young Swallows preparing to migrate. © Ian Rotherham

Don't take Kestrels for granted

At *The Star* we've had information from the British Trust for Ornithology about problems for one of our most familiar birds of prey, the Kestrel (or '*Wind-hover*'). In South Yorkshire we've had a particular attachment to the Kestrel ever since the Barry Hines book *A Kestrel for a Knave* and then the film *KES*. The title refers to the fact that in medieval times, with a strict 'pecking' order in falconry, the Kestrel was the only bird that a Knave at the Royal Court was allowed to '*fly*'. Set and filmed around Barnsley, it tells the story of a young boy and his life, set against the South Yorkshire landscape and his pet Kestrel. Not a '*hawk*' but a '*falcon*' the Kestrel is one of our most 'common' birds of prey, but whilst other species are generally recovering it is having a

rough patch. The British Trust for Ornithology, or BTO for those who wish to show off, is the main research organisation in Britain for the study of birds and their status; their breeding, wintering, migration, and trends. Their work and that of their network of unpaid volunteers provides baseline information to help guide conservation policy, *etc*. The BTO are so concerned about a decline in Kestrel numbers and breeding success that they have added it to their *Nest Record Scheme Concern* list. Information from BTO monitoring programmes is then sent to the Government's conservation advisory body, the Joint Nature Conservation Committee (or JNCC for short). Kestrels used to be a common sight, hovering over motorway and other roadside verges and grassy banks on the lookout for insects, small mammals, lizards, small birds and the like, but they have now been added to the special list with only twenty other species. Numbers dropped dramatically between the mid-1970s and the 1990s, probably due to agricultural intensification, but then appeared to have stabilised. Now it seems that breeding Kestrels are rearing only 3 chicks rather than 4 or 5 per brood.

This makes you consider how we can take things for granted; one problem for nature conservation (in my humble opinion) being that we often declare a crisis and call for action when it is way too late to do much. A bit like when I've written about invasive species that can cause damage to native wildlife, we often wait until they are really well-established before taking any action. By then it may well be too late and cost millions of pounds, yet we don't seem to learn. So the Kestrel has joined a select list of bird species considered to be at risk. These include a number of surprises such as Moorhen, Pied Wagtail, Grey Wagtail, Dunnock (or Hedge Sparrow), Willow Warbler and both House Sparrow and Starling, along with birds such as Barn Owl (that has recovered compared to a few years ago but still not totally secure).

Other birds at risk include Bullfinch, Linnet, Corn Bunting (now very rare in our area), Skylark and Yellowhammer. The main reason for the declines in these typical birds of the countryside and the urban-fringe is the loss of wildlife habitat due to the farming intensification that occurred in the 1970s, 1980s, and 1990s. Ironically a lot of this has now stopped, or at least the situation has not got much worse, so the rate of loss has slowed down. So it seems crazy that local individuals still feel it is ok to plough up the habitat of these species, like the Oakes Park orchid meadows in south Sheffield, or to destroy Water Vole and Great Crested Newt habitat (apparently with the knowledge of the agent of the owner, the Environment Agency) at Woodhouse Washlands Nature Reserve, and that nobody seems prepared or able to do anything about it. These important wildlife habitats are ours and are increasingly under threat and vulnerable (confirmed by the BTO report). Supposedly protected under European Legislation, but cast your eye around the region and you'll see similar and totally unnecessary losses on YOUR doorstep. Ask then who cares and who is taking action?? If you find out, let me know!

The English Turkey: Anyone for Roast Bustard?

The Great Bustard. From a Victorian print

The Corncrake, a once common bird of traditional cornfields and meadows, declined with intensive farming in the1940s and 1950s – its loss sudden and catastrophic. Not only did it disappear, but it was erased from the common memory. Now you see it, now you don't; as simple as that. In recent years, with sterling efforts from the RSPB, the Corncrake is holding its own and maybe even recovering in its strongholds of the far Western Isles of Scotland. They still pass through our region on migration, but this is in secrecy and mostly at night. It would be nice to see them back as breeding birds, and I hear rumours of sightings. Our last official records were from around Totley and

Dore in Sheffield in the late 1940s or early 1950s. However, I suspect that some of you out there have other recollections. The recent publication on the Frecheville area brought out some memories of this bird. So let me know if you recall Corncrakes anywhere across the *Sheffield Star* region; and also what did you call them. I gather there were local names, but often these are not written down and are lost. Have you seen or heard Corncrakes more recently?

I've been researching the history of another farmland bird from the past, the Great Bustard. I've no records from our region, but they certainly occurred in the great lowland sheep-walks beyond Doncaster in the Yorkshire East Riding. There's even a '*Bustard Farm*' at Great Driffield where the last Yorkshire Bustard attempted to breed and was shot. Incidentally, the Great Bustard was a highly-valued game bird before the introduction of the Turkey from North America. I have records of birds in feast menus from the Earls of Northumberland at their great house in Alnwick, but gathered from their estates in East Yorkshire. Almost certainly they would have occurred at least occasionally in our region, and certainly in Nottinghamshire, in the wide open heaths and commons of the medieval landscape. For us, they would have been a rare winter visitor. Now with a reintroduction programme in the south of England, I wonder if we will ever get them back. Now that would be exciting!! It is not beyond the bounds of possibility either. Only a week ago I saw a Red Kite drift over the A1 near Grantham and yet ten years ago that would have been inconceivable. So you just never know.

I was recently asked to open the official launch of a new local book; on the day Neil Warnock couldn't make it, so the locals had me instead! I gather the book is almost '*sold out*'. It is called '*Around the Nab – Local History Memories of Frecheville, Birley, Charnock and Basegreen*' and is all about the local people and history of Frecheville. Sponsored by the Heritage Lottery Fund the project has been the brainchild of local lady Chris Taylor. The project gathered local memories of the area and its recent rural past. It is the type of countryside we take for granted but that too often has been swept away. A dynamic group of local residents and former residents have carried out grassroots research with support from Hallam University's own Professor Melvyn Jones and his wife Joan, and co-ordinated by Christine Handley and former Hallam student Jennifer Argent. They have visited archives and local records centres, interviewed local people and then wrote and produced a great local history. The book has been incredibly popular, and though I say it is nearly '*sold out*', it is actually free. But what I do mean is that they have almost all gone! You might just get one from the local library or the Frecheville Community Centre. Anyway, do rush out to read a copy and you'll find out loads of things about the area, including on p39 the Corncrakes that used to call in the meadows and cornfields. The local kids could make a noise with dried grass and a comb that would make the Corncrakes call out to them. Now can anybody beat that??!

Land Rails and Nettle Peggies

The request for memories of Corncrakes brought some quick responses, so I'm hoping to hear more over the next few weeks. Paul West emailed to say: '*I was pleased to read about Corncrakes in the Star. I moved from Sheffield to the village of Storrs near Stannington in 1967 at the age of 10. For years in the warm summer evenings we would hear this strange sound like a rusty gate. At the time I had no idea what it was, being a stranger to the countryside. Looking back I can see that the farmer who had that field was not up with the times; this field had weeds and even to my city-bred eye looked different to the other farms in the area. I cannot put an exact date on when they last lived in the area but it must have been in the mid nineteen-seventies. Rather strangely I did hear a Corncrake in the same area in the early eighties on an unusually warm January night and it always puzzled me. I suppose it was a lone and confused bird returning the place of its birth. It would not surprise me that there are other Corncrakes recorded in the Bradfield area as due to the terrain intensive farming is difficult and even now there are pockets of land that are not heavily used.*' The call, of course, is the territorial and perhaps contact vocals as the male defends his patch. Apparently you can get a good response from a bird by imitating the call using a stick over notched piece of wood, or as at Frecheville,

with dried grass and a comb. The wonderful farmland around Stannington and Bradfield was, as Paul rightly says, much less vulnerable to intensification and mechanisation. Eventually it did of course change and the Corncrake was doomed.

Corncrake or Land Rail. From a Victorian print

Then across to the eastern side, Barrie Hicklin wrote in to say that he has no personal recollection of these elusive birds. However, his late father recalled seeing or hearing them as a common bird around Harthill. This was in the 1920s and 1930s, when he was a young man. Also very interesting is that the local name for Corncrake in Harthill village was '*Nettle Peggies*'. Now that is really helpful as I'm sure the Corncrake or Land Rail did have local names. There must be others out across the region, or maybe other villages that used this name too. The call is an incredibly distinctive '*crake, crake, crake*', and is heard both during the day and at night. It is described by writers in the early 1900s as scarcely distinguishable from the sound of the sharpening of a scythe on a whetstone. However, they also suggested that the call needed no description – as everyone would be familiar with it! I suspect very few people today will have heard either a scythe being sharpened on a whetstone (and if anybody has then do let me know) or a Corncrake. It is also both interesting and encouraging to read in early bird-watching books of the 1920s that Corncrakes were known to have declined and increased again previously. By the 1920s, the collapse in Corncrake numbers in the south of England was being attributed to mechanisation of farming and the change from hand cutting of hay and corn, and in the 1940s this same trend hit our region too.

The Wild Side of Tinsley Towers

Tinsley Towers. © Ian Rotherham

Now you see them, now you don't. It is funny how things turn out and how they change. In the last few months there's been a lot said about two big issues affecting our region – so far I've made no comment. The first concerns the famous twin cooling towers by Tinsley Viaduct and I want to establish some early history of the '*Save the Towers Campaign*'; it goes back longer than you might think!! Growing up in Sheffield's dirty 1960s I hated them as everything that appalled me about industry and pollution. Yet now, and many people don't feel this way, I am quite fond of them. Coming back to Sheffield from a meeting in Leeds, they tell me I'm home, and so did the stainless steel bull until it migrated. (Anybody know where it's gone??) But this is more than a home-coming beacon. In the early 1990s demolition was first mooted, but it turned out that we had the rare and protected Peregrine Falcon roosting on the towers, loving the open cliff-like environment. I was approached by a local businessman offering to pay for a steel nesting-platform and erection by steeplejacks. He'd seen this on TV at a power station in Derby and wanted the same for Sheffield. Imagine that, our very own nesting Peregrines in the heart of one of Europe's biggest industrial areas. My other idea was to have nest pictures from a remote camera direct to the big screen at the Meadowhall Food Oasis. The idea was that if you really wanted to get people involved in and

aware of wildlife across the region, this would be the way. To cut a long story short, after letters to the power company that owned the towers, and features on local radio and in the papers, nothing happened. The company said no, realising that if the Peregrines nested then the Towers would, in effect, be protected habitat, and they certainly didn't want that. Nearly twenty years on the Towers are still there and it seems a wasted opportunity.

My other suggestions at the time were to combine the conservation project with a major landscape artwork. We were going to paint the towers brick red and have giant Bill and Ben constructed over them, with a Little Weed in the middle. Who says I've no taste in art? Eat your heart out '*Angel of the North*', watch for '*Bill and Ben over Tinsley*'. A suggestion from my colleague Geoff Cartwright was that they were painted as huge flower-vases and mega plastic Daffodils placed in them. Now that's just silly!! Of course, about 18 months later, after this original article was written, they've gone!

Lost medieval woodland at Tinsley Park

Last week I mentioned the Sheffield Airport at Tinsley. It seems now the airport never really '*took off*' and so is '*permanently grounded*'. I used the Sheffield Airport when it went to Europe and it was good; much more environmentally sound than driving to Manchester or East Midlands. It was small, very user-friendly and had a baggage trolley rather than a baggage retrieval conveyor-belt! Landing was '*interesting*' with the short runway and not for the nervous; the planes small, rather like a single-decker bus with wings with a rubber-band propeller. Alas no more.

I worked for Sheffield City Council when the airport was proposed and developed. As City Ecologist I raised some issues and looking back there were others that we failed to address. Interestingly there were no objections on archaeological heritage grounds except that my colleague, Clive Hart, pointed out that the site was probably linked to England's greatest Dark Ages battle Brunanburh, at which in 937 AD King Athelstan subdued the Northumbrians, the Welsh, and the Irish. The TV Historian Michael Wood described this area as the '*Vietnam of*

Anglo-Saxon England', and the battle was described in the *Annals of Ulster* as '*immense, lamentable and horrible and desperately fought*' and it was noted that '*never before in this island was an army put to such great slaughter by the sword…*' This was followed by pursuit and annihilation throughout the nearby valleys and the southerners extinguished their defeated foes. Five kings and many other nobles plus probably thousands of ordinary soldiers were killed, both sides suffering huge losses. Apparently the area was strewn with both weapons and splendid treasures abandoned and lost; so do keep your eyes skinned when you're out and about!

How the valley-bottom wet woodland might have looked at Catcliffe. © Ian Rotherham

The setting for this cataclysmic event was the extensive swampy, lowland areas around Whiston and Catcliffe, and then Tinsley Wood, still a mile across when Joseph Hunter wrote of it in 1831. In medieval times this was a great deer park that was then split in two; half farmland and half coppice wood. This latter was to supply firstly charcoal for the region's emerging industry and then pit props for deep mines. By the late 1980s, there was a surprisingly rich and diverse ecology – the area's best urban wildlife site, but mostly behind British Steel's fences and a hidden asset. I think today much of the remaining woodland with its coppice trees and eighteenth century bell-pits would be recognised as of huge archaeological significance. However, at the time nothing was said and this aspect was not realised. As the imperative for a Sheffield Airport took hold, it was decided to opencast the area and to remove with that around five hundred years of industrial pollution (some of it very '*hot*' stuff).

A campaign by local people and with support form Melvyn Jones and Mike Wild at the then Sheffield Polytechnic helped us remove substantial areas of woodland from the proposals and to also save the medieval parish boundary and wood banks. However, the pressure was on for the rest and the importance of the airport was such that the large area of coppice Bluebell wood was destroyed, for the greater, long-term good. Some material was '*rescued*' and money was provided to establish the Blackburn Meadows Nature Reserve, so some good did come of this. But a very large and hugely biodiverse and historic site was utterly destroyed. At the time it was argued very strongly that the airport was so important to Sheffield, that this small sacrifice of ecology (and now I realise archaeology), simply had to be made. Well time passes and it seems now that maybe it wasn't so important after all. Very strange this, because we were told that it was absolutely critical for the future commercial and political success of Sheffield. So was it or wasn't it? The woodland had survived, according to eminent historian Michael Wood, since before Domesday – maybe 1,500 years; this was lost to the airport that survived around fifteen years. Does any of this make sense?

Kingfishers on the up

British Waterways is the main organisation that conserves and manages our navigable waterways – mostly canals, and they undertake an annual wildlife survey. The results for this year have just come out and the news is good. In particular, that gem of the waterway, the Kingfisher, has done well. This is the fourth year of the survey which helps to track the biodiversity of canals and rivers. In many areas such as across our region, these are vital wildlife corridors. They help sustain populations of both common and threatened species, and are great for people too. Monitoring the extensive network is a job for both volunteers and professionals, so the waterways survey organisers encourage people visiting and using rivers and canals to take part and to send in their sightings. In 2007, across the country, there were around 4,000 wildlife records sent in. Of course the watercourses and their wildlife extend into and through urban centres like Doncaster, Sheffield and Rotherham. The excitement is then that this draws a rich variety of wildlife right into the city heartland; bringing people and nature together. An important focus for this year's survey was the kingfisher. This bird is a useful indicator of good water quality and a healthy ecosystem. Like us, they are at the top of the '*food chain*'; so in the 1960s with DDT pesticide pollution, it was birds like Kingfisher and Grey Heron that were poisoned and died. This was bad for them, but an important warning for us. We've changed our ways now and birds such as Kingfisher, Great Crested Grebe (still on the Ewden Valley reservoirs according to Michael Parker), and of course Heron, are now doing well. Indeed Paul License has reported regular sightings of Herons around the River Don, and even one perched on the roof of flats overlooking the Don on Nursery Street. He also heard rather than saw a Kingfisher down by Neepsend.

A Mute Swan on one of the local rivers. © Ian Rotherham

So the good news is that over 300 Kingfishers were spotted in this year's British Waterways' survey, an increase of nearly five percent on 2006. This is despite the wet summer. (Maybe Kingfishers liked the wet weather). The British Waterways' team of professional ecologists also report good stable populations of Kingfishers across the network of rivers and canals in both urban and rural waterways. Responding to the survey results, a number of habitat improvement projects for Kingfishers are planned to help support these important populations. You can find out more about all this from www.waterscape.com. It will also give you details of the survey results, and information on the best places to spot Kingfishers and other

wildlife. As part of the annual survey, British Waterways also run a photographic competition, and local wildlife enthusiast Steve Ibbotson was one of the winners. Apparently '*The lightning quick reactions and keen eye sight of a Sheffield man when he spotted a magnificent Kingfisher darting above the water at the Shropshire Union Canal in Ellesmere have been rewarded with a top place in a national photographic competition.*' The competition challenged waterway visitors to capture the distinctive bird on camera. This is no mean feat as Kingfishers fly at speeds up to 40mph which means a flash of electric blue is all that many are lucky enough to glimpse. Steve Ibbotson's photograph was chosen above other entries because British Waterways' judges, including ecologists, felt it captured the grace and stunning beauty of the Kingfisher perfectly. He beat off stiff competition from other budding wildlife photographers around the UK and his efforts have been rewarded with a Waterscape.com goodie bag. So well done Steve!!

Along with Sheffield's famous River Don Red Deer, Otters have been spotted by a resident whose flat looks out on to the river. The landlady of the Riverside Pub on Mowbray Street has also reported activity. Apparently conservation workers have helped by constructing artificial '*holts*' from old branches and rubble and it has worked a treat. It may have looked a mess (a jumble of logs and branches) but it clearly did its job, and the wildlife is less concerned by aesthetics.

Enjoying Local Nature

One of the many good things about our region is the ease with which you can see wildlife. It is one of the best places to view varied wildlife habitats and a rich diversity of nature; mostly seen for free. We are surrounded by nature reserves, especially in the eastern lowlands, and of course to the west is the magnificent Peak National Park. Whether you want to just experience nature and landscape, or to see particular birds or flowers, these offer a dazzling variety. Most are also reasonably close to public transport, though perhaps not so easy as in my youth. Taking the bus out to Ewden, or Bradfield, or to Castleton or Derwent, all for around two old pence was pretty good! Nowadays, most of us rely on a car, which is a shame.

However, and a great thing about our region, is that closer to home there are lots of good places and pleasurable walks. We have walks in Sheffield along the valleys and through the associated woodlands, such as Ecclesall Woods on the Sheaf, or the extensive Wharncliffe Woods on the Don between Sheffield and Barnsley. In the east, there are walks along the River Don and the canals, such as at Sprotborough for example, or around Askern. Again in the area around Askern and Moss, there are exciting green lands and other tracks suitable for walking, horse-riding, and mountain bikes. Go for a quiet walk along any of these and you will see a good range of the commoner resident and winter visitor birds. These are ancient tracks with old trees and medieval hedges and banks; a wonderful landscape and rich wildlife habitat. It is interesting to have a favoured walk and make notes on what you see. After a few visits you begin to know where and when to look for certain birds or even mammals, and there will be changes with weather or the seasons too. Your records can also build up to be a useful and possibly important catalogue of the local wildlife. You never know when your site might come under threat; your notes may help safeguard its future.

Woodhouse Washlands sunset. © Ian Rotherham

If you live around south Rotherham or south-east Sheffield, then you can very easily visit Woodhouse Washlands Yorkshire Wildlife Trust Nature Reserve. It is open to the public and free to all, with well made paths and easy access. I've had reports of good numbers of common birds such as Robins, and watch out for the winter thrushes, Redwing and Fieldfare, feasting with local Blackbirds on Hawthorns and

other berry bushes. On the River Rother, here and close-by, you get views of specialist wetland birds; Moorhens and Coots and the flash of a Kingfisher. There've been twelve Goosanders at Woodhouse, a record for the Reserve, and Snipe on the marshes too. Here and at similar sites it is worth watching for flocks of both Lapwing and the less common Golden Plover; the latter breed in small numbers on high moorlands. However, in winter they form huge flocks around lowland wetlands and arable farmland. The area around North Anston was favoured, but Old Moor and Potteric Carr are excellent too. The flocks, numbering hundreds or more, wheel across our region's skies, unseen by most people, but worth looking out for. Lapwing, in particular, can be seen almost anywhere, forming quite tight flocks with myriad wings giving a distinctive flickering effect.

However, if you are gazing skywards in search of flocks of birds, then watch out for long lines of seagulls flying high and a long way between feeding and roosting sites. In winter, several species come inland and take full advantage of water supply reservoirs across the region. If you are in one of the areas through which they pass, then expect large numbers going over. They appear to be flying in a 'v' formation and often very high, so everyone assumes they must be geese; more exciting but less likely. We do get geese over the region but I'll say more about that in the future. Latest news is of Dippers right in the middle of Sheffield on the River Don. Top that!

Wild about South Yorkshire

Here in South Yorkshire, and the surrounding areas of North Derbyshire and North Notts., we are well placed to see exciting wildlife. Both on the doorstep and further afield, but conveniently close, we have some of Britain's best wildlife sites. So if you are thinking about where to go, or perhaps where to take the kids or grandchildren, you are really spoiled for choice. At this time of year it is worth trying sites that offer summer specials – say the Derbyshire Dales or Yorkshire's Magnesian limestone for grassland wild flowers and butterflies. For example an excellent site is Maltby Common in (as you might expect) Maltby near Rotherham. This is a Yorkshire Wildlife Trust Nature

Reserve and is freely open to the public. On a sunny day you can expect a rich variety of insects especially butterflies, and the speciality of the site, its limestone wild flowers including a range of orchids. You will also hear and see a range of birds such as Willow Warbler, Whitethroat, and plenty of more common finches, titmice, and thrushes, *etc*. Amongst the mammals, look out for signs of Roe Deer and even Muntjac. You can get exact details of how to get there from the Yorkshire Wildlife Trust web site.

Out to the west all the Derbyshire Dales (on Carboniferous Limestone) are well worth a visit. The grassland flowers are very rich, and again there is the chance of some exciting butterflies too. The dale-side woodlands tend to be either Sycamore-dominated or Ash. They are often incredibly species-rich but surprisingly not very old. Many are only 200-300 years old and represent the re-colonisation of the dales by trees when sheep-grazing stopped. There are smaller pockets of wonderful Lime Woods, some of the best in Britain, but perhaps we'll talk about them some other time. Out in the sunlit dales this is the time to look for Common Blue Butterflies, with Meadow Browns, Gatekeepers, Small Heaths and many others. Try classic sites like Lathkill Dale or Monks Dale. Most are easy to get to by car or even by public transport or bike. You can get a potted version of the limestone dale experience along one of the trails such as the Monsal Trail, from Hassop Station or from Bakewell Station. This is easy walking and will provide plenty of wildflowers, butterflies, glorious views and the chance of plenty of birds too. The old railway lines with their limestone chippings have a flora very typical of the Dales region.

Bakewell and the gateway to the Derbyshire Dales. © Ian Rotherham

If you're in Barnsley then a trip to Worsbrough Mill Country Park is a must. The park itself has pleasant walks round the old reservoir that supplied water to the Barnsley Canal. The open water turns up a good range of ducks and other waterfowl; the willow carr holds other interest with warblers and other birds such as Long-tailed tits in abundance. Open water holds Little Grebes with their anxious high-pitched whittering as they feed their broods of youngsters. All the wetland areas have interesting wild flowers, and there are several areas of rather nice grassland too. Look out for woodland butterflies such as Speckled Wood, Orange Tip, Green-veined White, and in the open areas Comma, Small Tortoiseshell, Red Admiral and all the Browns. The disused railway line is good for these as well and has lots of interesting wildflowers. If you have time then take a walk to the nearby woods, downstream of the park. They are wonderful with old trees from the long-abandoned Worsbrough Park that was attached to the old hall. Look out for some monster Oaks and Ash trees too. In this area there's a good chance of Great Spotted Woodpecker and Nuthatch. Cast your eyes down and the ancient woodland wild flowers are good too. Look out for grasses like Wood Melick and Wood Millet, and the Dog's Mercury; such a good indicator of an old woodland. If you are near the streamside then watch for Kingfisher, this is a good area for them. You can finish with a walk by the old canal, but keep a good distance from the fishermen; best not disturb their concentration, and the hooks flying through the air are worth avoiding too! But here you should look out for

Dandelion clocks. © Ian Rotherham

the damsels and dragons, or at least Damselflies and Dragonflies. This is a good spot and you should see several different species. Basically if the insect is small and the wings rest along its back then you are looking at a Damselfly and if it is large and at rest the wings stick out sideways, then it is a Dragonfly. We'll touch on these in more detail some other time!

Right Here, Right Now

Climate change is all the news so it must be real; not '*what if*', but '*when and how much*'. Thanks to DLA Piper I was fortunate to get a ticket for Al Gore's *Cooling the Planet* in Sheffield a couple of weeks ago. Unlike my colleagues who are real journalists and were not allowed to stay, as a researcher in environmental change my credentials were not to do with this column. So I was privileged indeed. My take on the theme is in summary a bit like the old horror films – *be afraid, be very afraid*!! Not that former Vice-President Gore was negative; he wasn't. In fact he was very upbeat in highlighting not only the dire state of the planet, but his optimism that business opportunities and enlightened politicians can address and resolve the worst issues. He drew attention to the major economic opportunities presented by the need to address global environmental change – technological and engineering solutions that could be good for centres of expertise such as Sheffield. This idea, of course, isn't new; it has been one of the main drivers for corporate environmental management for a couple of decades, but the presentation was passionate, intelligent and informed, with a surprisingly confident and clever stage-presence. Gore seemed relaxed and far more at ease than the figure of failed presidential campaigns; with some asides worthy of a stand-up comedian.

No, my fear is that the great and the good, present in abundance at the event, will not take the whole thing sufficiently seriously to solve the problems, and certainly not in the time-scale needed. I do know many of the people and unless there's a sudden and dramatic conversion on the Road to Damascus, I don't feel too optimistic. Part of this is because I really don't think they understand. They probably don't want to destroy the planet, but they also hope that it can be solved by planting a few trees, driving a slightly smaller 4x4, and hoping it won't all be too

inconvenient or affect the winter ski holiday. In the meantime they can rub shoulders with one of the few great politicians and world leaders of the last twenty years and feel pretty good that they are doing their bit. Well I'm sorry but it isn't good enough and it won't do. Not only that, but there really isn't a lot of time to play with. So my questions to the great and good of Sheffield and South Yorkshire are: do you really think that you understand and then are you doing enough? Can you really look into the mirror and still have a clear conscience? (If you see nothing at all then avoid garlic!)

The trouble is that I've experienced 30-40 years of indecision and dithering by the region's great and good, and with a few exceptions they really don't understand the nature of the task; the sheer enormity of the commitment and the challenge. A handful of gifted local authority officers, a very few committed councillors and MPs, and a disappointingly few local business-persons, are exceptions proving the rule. To find a genuine environmental champion you'd have to go back to Alderman Graves, a very long time ago. A few have dabbled but not lasted the course; with those that have, are or were generally considered a bit eccentric by their colleagues. Support to environmental services and initiatives in the region's local authorities have, over the years, followed this lack of priority and suffered a poverty of comprehension. For readers in Doncaster, Barnsley, and Rotherham, for example, *your* countryside services and country parks staff have recently been cut to the bone. I wonder how that squares with our region being a beacon for the rest of the world in terms of green issues and environmental responsibility. I'd love to have been able to talk directly to Mr Gore and find out what he sees behind the rhetoric. His was perhaps the most significant and important message ever delivered to an audience in the region, possibly in the UK. I hope we take it seriously, because if we are a beacon of light for the environment, then God help the rest!

Wildlife depends our good husbandry of the environment; Gatekeeper Butterfly on Marjoram. © Ian Rotherham

One Down and a Few Billion to Go

Well it seems we've done a bit of good and my article on Green Oaks Park in Totley Rise helped save an old Oak tree. So there we are, job done; one down and a few billion to work on. I've had many letters and emails about the article and the problems that local people face. Part of the issue seems to be that when key decisions are made, even small ones may affect doorstep quality of life, and ordinary people are missed out. There are endless consultations on broad issues but when actual decisions are made it's back to 'business as usual', short-term economics and development. Real greening and commitment to genuine sustainable development, which must include the other living organisms with which we share the planet, still seem way off; despite tokenism and rhetoric.

So back to last week's theme and Mr Gore's landmark speech in Sheffield; not only an audience of the influential, the great and good, but a shared platform too. And it was encouraging to hear keynote speeches from senior colleagues in bodies like *Yorkshire Forward*, but come on guys, this is an organisation that has been notoriously slow off the mark on the environment. Transformed? I hope so, but I await proof. You're a bit late to the party! Those responsible for Oakes Park in Norton were there too. What is their legacy to Sheffield's environment? Will their names be remembered and respected like Alderman Graves or Gerald Haythornthwaite? I suspect not. One problem is that climate change is not merely about carbon, renewable energy and efficiency, and greenhouse gases; it is also about ***ecosystem function***. This is how the environment delivers the services we require in terms of water, energy, food, habitation, landscape, weather, nature and wildlife, quality of life, health, *etc*. Importantly though it isn't just these. There's a lot more to ecosystem function. The state of the environment affects the ability of the ecosystems to respond to change; as they always have over the millennia. One of the problems now, and look around the region when you're out and about to see what I mean, is that the basic ecological systems are very patchy, and what's left is mostly in pretty poor shape. There are exciting projects like the *Moors for the Future* in the Peak District or *Potteric Carr Yorkshire Wildlife Trust Nature Reserve* with its massive new wetlands, or the *RSPB Dearne Valley* complex, but what about the rest in-between? A message from the Al Gore event was surely that everybody and every site, no matter how small or insignificant, must be a part of the bigger picture. Obviously the big and prestigious plans and sites are hugely important, but then in managing climate, water (drought and flood), and biodiversity and the rest, everything is '*in*'. So the Oak tree at Totley Rise, to the Acers (according to respected environmentalist Marion Tylecote) recently felled around Barker's Pool, or the wildflower meadows ploughed up in Oakes Park or abandoned in Graves Park, or the vast areas of moorland west of Sheffield needlessly ploughed up and despoiled for personal gain over a 20-year period, each one in its own unique way contributes another nail in the coffin of regional sustainability. What's more, each person responsible for these individual acts has made a personal statement and a special and individual contribution to global climate change at our regional level.

Peak District moorlands; huge areas were ploughed up by a single landowning family in the 1980s and 1990s. © Ian Rotherham

In a large part, what I'm arguing for is a greater degree of respect – for the environment, for the community, and for the future. This doesn't just mean wildlife and nature, but for our built heritage too. I understand from Marion that it is planned to demolish more Victorian buildings around Cambridge Street, including Listed Buildings; surely not? Is that really what local people want? All the actions I've noted, and there are many, many more (believe me I can send you a list!), have either unwittingly in some cases, and maliciously in others, contributed to a huge problem. I wonder how many of those that have done this will now try to repair the damage. I would guess not many.

Wild around the Ewden Valley

The Ewden Valley or '*Valley of the yew trees*' is one of my favourite wildlife watching areas. So it was a pleasant surprise when a letter from Michael Parker of Deepcar arrived to reawaken a few memories. He was asking about a number of sightings of birds of prey, and all in one afternoon. This is actually typical of the Ewden Valley, a wonderful and rich site that makes you proud to come from around here. I had chance to discuss the sighting with two experienced colleagues and we are pretty much in agreement! Michael and a friend had seen several birds, in at least three separate groups, down the Valley and thought they might be Buzzards. If only life was so simple! The first two points to make are: 1) that the Ewden Valley is a brilliant area for birds of prey. It used to be my old stomping ground and anything can and does turn up. 2) Birds of

prey in flight are notoriously difficult to identify with certainty when the view is not close straightforward. So we made some suggestions. The bird described and drawn by Michael seems most like Common Buzzard, which is now well-established in the area. Buzzards are very variable in colour and markings with patches of white and brown. The other birds could be the same and he may have been observing a winter roost. Many birds of prey come together in the afternoon to roost at a favoured location. However, they could also be pairs establishing breeding territories. Calls are always difficult to describe but Buzzards are very vocal with usually with a loud mewing. In fact call and flight are the main clues. This often doesn't help the novice as they expect a bird to look like it does in a guidebook or on TV; they don't! No, in most cases you have to rely on behaviour (including calls) and an overall feel for the species. Birdwatchers call this '*jizz*' and it comes with experience.

People always think size is the key, but it is misleading and especially so in flight unless there is a known bird or other object to give scale. Female Sparrowhawk is smaller but can look and behave, to the less experienced observer, rather like a Buzzard. So some or even all of Michael's birds could have been Sparrowhawks. However, the male Sparrowhawk is noticeably smaller (reasonably obvious with pairs of birds flying together) and is grey–blue in colour on the back and mantle. So where does this leave us (or rather Michael and his friends)? The combined sightings could easily be a mixture of say a pair of Buzzards higher up the Valley and a couple of pairs of Sparrowhawks around the plantation woodlands lower down. Again they could be displaying over potential breeding territories. A further complication is the potential for the Sparrowhawk's larger cousin, the Goshawk. That is less likely, but it is possible that at least one of the sightings was this species.

Watercolour of a Common Pheasant. © Ian Rotherham

He also saw what he thought (correctly) were Pheasants up by the old quarries not far from the moorland edge. However, he was put off by the fact that they were rather small and brown and kept huddled together and apparently not afraid of people (I hope they learn soon!!). They were ordinary Pheasants but youngsters. The rearing pens close-by explains their lack of fear. I also think that Michael's possible Black Grouse he reported from the same location were actually Red Grouse. They can look very dark. There has been a reintroduction project for Black Grouse in the Peak District but they are still extremely rare. His final question for me was concerning two rather large and oddly-coloured ducks on the River Don at Oughtibridge. Absolutely right Michael they are Mallard hybrids; known in the trade as '*Heinz 57s*'. So there we are, all questions answered, and I hope correctly. Fingers crossed! One final observation came in from George Diprose: a Dipper on the River Sheaf near Heeley Baths. That is really good to hear.

Steve Cross from Walkley wrote in with more sightings of birds of prey from the Ewden and Morehall area. He confirmed Buzzard reports and whilst fishing has also seen Sparrowhawk and probably Goshawk. Steve has also seen birds of prey soaring high over Parkwood Springs. To be honest these could be almost anything. Birds of prey love thermals and will rise a huge distance. These will sometimes be local birds, and sometimes ones on migration. (Beware of other species that at this sort of distance look like raptors – for example gulls or Grey Heron!). However, he also told me about a really interesting observation of wagtails roosting. Not

everyone realises this but we have three species of wagtails common to the region. Of these, two (Pied Wagtail and Grey Wagtail) I'd expect to see regularly; the third (Yellow Wagtail) is quite rare except in the White Peak of Derbyshire. Now what was particularly interesting about Steve's observation was a night-time roost of 50-70 wagtails around the furnaces at CORUS Stockbridge works. As he suggests, they are attracted by the warmth. I'm assuming that this is mostly in winter; although he has seen evidence of the birds nesting and young birds being accidentally lost due to work on site. Communal roosts are quite common in some birds and especially in winter or when on migration. I've seen a roost of around 500 Pied Wagtails around the Cultural Industries Quarter in the centre of Sheffield, and even on the roof of the Hallam University City Campus buildings.

Pied Wagtails.

Steve thinks his birds are mainly Pied Wagtails (with which I agree) with some Yellow Wagtails (about which I am very doubtful). The reasons for my disagreement over the Yellow Wagtails are firstly they are a summer visitor that migrates to us. The other species do migrate too, but many visit in winter and we have them with us as residents, i.e. all year round. As I said earlier, the Yellow is quite uncommon in our region except in summer in the White Peak. Otherwise odd ones turn up, but not in numbers; so why the confusion? Well, the Grey Wagtail has a lot of yellow on it, and this is the main image when you see it. Not helpful!! The Grey is common along our urban rivers, is a very noticeable and striking bird that is bigger and has a longer tail than the Pied. Anyway, my money is on Steve's roost being a mix of Pied Wagtails and Grey Wagtails (which are yellow!!). Why do birds roost communally? Well there are many reasons. One might be that they are all attracted to the most favourable (warm/secure/sheltered) sites. Another is company and security in numbers; a bit like people. It is also believed that they interact socially, meet potential mates, and importantly exchange information about good feeding areas. It's just like going down the pub and then off to a curry house or chippie…!

There's plenty to get excited about. Unusual winds during spring brought spectacular visitors to eastern England; perhaps Cranes were the most striking. It would be great to think of them fully re-established in Britain in the not-too-distant future. They've been down in East Anglia for a while, so imagine at Old Moor or somewhere similar. Wow, wouldn't that be something?!

The Common Crane from a Victorian print; now making a remarkable comeback

Another bird doing well is the Osprey. Following a spectacular recovery in Scotland over 30-40 years, a ten-year release programme at Rutland Water in Leicestershire has finally paid off. Following a courtship beginning last year, a pair of Ospreys is breeding at this major nature reserve. Dozens of young Ospreys were released into the wild over the period to form a breeding base. If the Red Kite reintroduction success is followed, then we can look forward to a massive increase of Ospreys in England, including our region. Wouldn't Ospreys in, say, the Derwent Valley or perhaps Ewden be a bit special? I wonder what the fishermen think. We've had them passing through on migration for quite a few years (Ospreys not fishermen!). In fact I remember one that sat on the church spire in Hayfield many years ago, and was seen up and down the Goyt Valley in the western Peak District. We're already getting very interesting birds turning up; and they can be seen almost anywhere. A few weeks ago, Paul Licence saw a young Kite out at Longshaw, and then only a month ago I saw a Buzzard pass lazily over the Dronfield by-pass. Ten years ago that would have been unbelievable. Recently a Hobby was reported from a garden in Gleadless, but from the description and its behaviour I think it was a male Sparrowhawk. But still very nice, sat on the hedge surveying the garden.

However, there's the other side of our environment too with damage to local Badger setts; sad when it is so avoidable and may even be a local authority or a sub-contractor. I can't say where because of obvious need to safeguard the animals. However, it was a sett that local business was trying to protect as part of a development, going to great lengths to follow legal process, protecting the site and feeding areas. This was to the point of developing a management plan to secure the Badgers' future habitat; yet someone has, totally illegally, removed by machine all the scrub vegetation on adjacent land. Disturbance this close, even accidental, is illegal with a potentially severe sentence; this should not happen.

Michael Parker wrote in with questions about Ewden Valley and the surrounding area. He was walking by the overflow between the Morehall and Broomhead reservoirs, when he saw what he thought was a Grebe. It was about a foot long and had a long, slender and sharply pointed beak, with outsized yellow legs, a long neck with a white throat, and a dark grey back. However, although he could see what he describes as bushy eyebrows, there was no ruff or crest; something you might expect in a Grebe. The bird was watching Michael watching it. When his attention was disturbed and he looked away, the bird disappeared. Despite carefully watching and scanning the area, it never reappeared. Okay, let's think about this one; there two likely Grebe species and I are sure that Michael is watching a Grebe. One is the Little Grebe or Dabchick, rather small, round and often reddish in colour. The other is the Great Crested Grebe; big, spectacular with the striking head-crests and the weird head-shaking courtship displays. Both species can be seen on the Ewden Valley Reservoirs, but the description doesn't really fit either of these, but on size alone we can dismiss the Dabchick. Of course the problem is the time of year, as after breeding the birds moult into their winter plumage, and that is what Michael is looking at. It could also be a young bird as well. The disappearing act is interesting too, Grebes being able to stay under water for quite a while, and swim a good distance too. I guess it slipped into bank-side vegetation and kept its head down. Whilst Michael was looking at the bird it probably felt the best ploy was to remain stationary, and pretend he couldn't see it. As soon as he turned away and lost eye-contact then it was off. They're not so daft! Michael wondered if a Pike might have taken the bird. Whilst I'm sure there are some in the reservoirs, I don't think that was the answer, it just hid.

He also raised an interesting question that one or two other people have asked about the impacts of the floods, so I'll deal with that here as well. Having watched a Grey Heron lazily fly down the Don Valley, and also noticed small Brown Trout in the Don at Deepcar, he wondered how long it would take for the River's fish-life to recover. I suspect not as long as you might think. Many river dwellers react to storm events by either sheltering (small invertebrates for example have evolved to hide away out of the current or to flatten themselves against rocks and vegetation), or to seek shelter in side-streams and

other areas relatively out of harm's way. It all depends on the size of the storm, but many of these creatures are remarkably resilient.

Great Crested Grebe. From an eighteenth century print

Award-winning wildlife site under threat

I was just getting ready to write an article about the good things in life; birds singing, and joys of spring, *etc.* then wham!! A message from old friend Roger Butterfield – and it all goes 'belly-up'. Not that it wasn't good to hear from him; rather the opposite. I have talked before about local champions for the region, and he is one of the unsung heroes. He's worked for Sheffield and the region's environment since before I can remember (and that's a long time!). A founder of the Hallam/Sheffield Conservation Volunteers, then Sheffield Environmental Training, and active in both Sorby Natural History Society and Sheffield Wildlife Trust. In fact he was a founder of the Sheffield City Wildlife Group that grew into SWT. So Roger does get around a bit!! No, the reason for the changed article was the message he sent: '*Proposal to build 16 houses on the wildlife garden at Abbeydale Hall*'. [Reference: 06/04408/OUT] Apparently, and this is all in the public domain, the owner of Abbeydale Hall, Mr G. Cunningham, has applied for planning permission to build sixteen houses in the part of the gardens formerly used as an environmental education resource (i.e. the wildlife garden and ponds restored by Sheffield Conservation Volunteers in the 1980s). The '*Expiry Date for Standard Consultations*' was

19th March 2007 (so I wonder why we only hear about this now. What on earth has happened to all the local networking by environmental groups? Doesn't anybody care anymore?!). However, and this is important, it is worth submitting comments even if you miss this deadline. You can view and comment on the proposals via the City Council's website at: http://tinyurl.com/3c2okr. I've included below the comments from Roger Butterfield (17th March 2007): '*In the 1980s, I was one of the hundreds of volunteers who spent many hours restoring the gardens at Abbeydale Hall. With support and encouragement from Sheffield City Council, our aim was to create an environmental education resource for use by schoolchildren and adults. I was very alarmed to hear that the current owner now wishes to build on the gardens. Having examined the plan titled "Outline Planning: Site plan" I cannot see how the development could possibly go ahead without completely destroying the ponds and other habitats and special features of the gardens. This is a relatively small site, with very limited vehicular access. Just getting materials and equipment on to the site would cause irrevocable damage to the gardens.*'

Now I, too, was involved in this site with the Local Friends Group and Sheffield Wildlife Action. It won conservation awards, had thousands of pounds of grant aid from the Environment Agency and equal amounts raised by volunteers. Tens of thousands of volunteer hours were spent restoring the Victorian ponds and crate a wonderful wildlife oasis. This haven for Kingfishers, for Woodpeckers, Bats, Badgers, Foxes, Herons, Newts, Frogs and Toads, for Sparrowhawks and woodland and meadow wildflowers, is under threat purely for personal gain and greed. It really is outrageous. The site also has a fantastic collection of large, mature trees, and yes they do have bat roosts.

Long-tailed Tits

But there is more. Until the last Conservative Government passed the Education Act, *this site belonged to us* – yes, you and me, the public of Sheffield. It was an environmental education base and a horticultural centre. The Act passed this schedule and protected '*Community Wildlife Area*' (the same status locally as a *Site of Scientific Interest*) to the responsibility and custodianship of *Sheffield College* at their Norton Centre. Believe it or not, the College first of all banned the volunteers from visiting and working on *their* site, closed the centre in the historic Abbeydale Hall, and yes, you've guessed it, flogged the lot to a local developer!! Now there's an educational example for the next generation. I can only wonder what Al Gore would say to that. Please do your bit and write or email in, telling Councillors and Planners to do their bit and save what is left of this wonderful site. The Council web site states that an Environmental Impact Assessment has not been requested!!! Why??

Wildlife on the doorstep

There's actually a bit of a debate going on in scientific circles at the moment, and believe it or not, wildlife in your garden is part of the issue. At Sheffield University there has been a uniquely interesting study called the *BUGS* or '*Biodiversity in Urban Gardens*' project. It has kept Sheffield right in the forefront of this topic, following the footsteps of Chris Baines, Oliver Gilbert and others back in the 1980s. One of the issues is to do with the importance of gardens for urban ecosystems and conservation, and in particular the questions of size and location. In other words does it matter how big or where your garden is? Now it appears that in terms of the bugs in your garden, hugely important in making the garden and urban ecosystems function, and often unseen and un-noticed, it doesn't make much difference. So all gardens, big and small, and no matter where they are, contribute to the urban ecosystem. However (and for me this is a *BIG* however!), for many of the types of wildlife that get gardeners really excited (birds, mammals, reptiles and amphibians, butterflies, dragonflies *etc*), size and location are massively important. It is true that anything and everything can and does turn up anywhere. (I remember a seabird called a Little Auk popping up on a very small garden pond in Gleadless back in the 1980s). But the likelihood gets much better for a big garden in a favourable location. As a gardener you can also do more with a larger plot.

Water Rail from a Victorian print; a rare garden visitor

For many years I ran wildlife gardening classes and this involved visits to the course-members' gardens; a good chance to nosey around and see what was what. Over the years I've assessed and commented on hundreds of gardens; and size and location do matter. This was brought back to me by a letter from Mike and Norma Jackson in Dore, Sheffield. In around forty years of wildlife gardening they've accumulated a list of seventy-five birds in the garden (including Snipe, Woodcock, Lesser Spotted Woodpecker, Cuckoo, Pied flycatcher, Arctic Redpoll, Brambling, Crossbill and Hawfinch) and another twenty-six species overhead. If that wasn't enough, they had a spectacular visitor last November: a Water Rail. For a week or so this exciting bird paraded around the pond and the stream (I'm presuming that this is a pretty large garden!), and across the lawn. Sadly, Friday 17th November was a sad day, as the Water Rail was found not only dead, but decapitated (Nature red in tooth and claw, *etc*). So '*who done it*'? Mike thinks a domestic cat, partly because the body wasn't found until the morning. I'm not sure as the decapitation is generally the hallmark of a bird of prey (they like the brains!), which perhaps abandoned the body as it was disturbed, and because it was too heavy to carry. My money is on an early-morning female Sparrowhawk or maybe even a Peregrine, you just never know; and they can be around quite early. If there are photographs, then

that would help further in the *Case of the Decapitated Water Rail*. However, the great thing about gardens is the unexpected. A couple of weeks ago Mike and Norma had a cock Pheasant strutting about their lawn; bird species number seventy-seven and a total of 103 with those flying over. (I've contacted the RSPB and Mike and Norma will be evicted next week and the garden made into a Nature Reserve). Now here's the rub. Paul Ardron recently saw a cock Pheasant on the lawn of the NATWEST Bank in Broomhill, in Sheffield, in the middle of the day. So anything can turn up anywhere. Wherever your garden is it can be a fantastic wildlife habitat, and of course it is special because it is yours. But if I were a gambler, then my money would be on Mike and Norma's garden on the edge of the Peak District moors and open countryside, to turn up numbers, species, and specials. Let me know what you get in your garden and what you think about size and location!

Wild in the Garden

Well it has been a busy couple of weeks. Not just for me but for the various birds in my wildlife garden. The feeders are literally heaving with baby Blue Tits, baby Great Tits, and loads of Goldfinches – with their wonderful varied and almost spluttering calls and chirrups. I think the tops are probably the family of great spotted woodpeckers that love both the nuts and the fat balls. They have to fight off a number of enormously fat Squirrels. It is actually surprising that the poor Squirrels can climb as far as the feeders; more surprising perhaps is that the feeders can support them. I wonder if you have noticed the increase in Wood Pigeons in the garden. They are now one of our most common and frequent garden birds; again pretty plump and hoovering up vast quantities of birdseed. Not that many years ago, they were still quite infrequent visitors to most city gardens. How times change.

Who's looking at you? Weasel. © Steve Smith

Our biggest triumph this year has been a brood of Blackbirds reared against all the odds, in a nest hidden behind a rambling rose on the garage wall. The parents have worked incredibly hard for a few weeks now. Firstly, there were innumerable flights in and out, semi-secretively, as material was collected for the nest. Then followed the period of quite as the female brooded on the eggs, after which all hell broke loose. There was an increasingly fervent flying back and forth with food for the nestlings. However, this is the time when there is a real risk of nest predation. Ever watchful, a Magpie noticed the action and began to take an undue interest in the site. Fortunately, the vegetation both provided cover and I suspect was too weak to support the Magpie (a large bird when you get them at close quarters). It was too close for comfort and the parent Blackbirds were beside themselves, calling and displaying. Their activity was ever more energetic as the black-and-white potential nest robber closed in. This went on for a day or so, and I think the babies were saved by the lack of easy access for the Magpie, but then by the rain. And boy did it rain. By the time it finished the Magpie had forgotten the nest, and the babies were ready to take the plunge and leave. Again, there was a near disaster. One of the baby Blackbirds perched out on top of a low bush was spied by our neighbour's cat *Stumpy*; a very friendly and characterful feline. However, a cat and a baby Blackbird are not a good mix (unless you happen to be the cat). The parents swung into action again and with a bit of timely human intervention *Stumpy's* intentions were thwarted, and the baby lived to twitter for another day.

So it has been all action, and at times quite nerve-racking. '*Nature red in tooth and claw*' is a great theory but when it is *your* baby Blackbirds, it does seem a bit harsh. Last but not least was the highlight of the week; and this really put the wind up the Blue Tits, Great Tits, and the Blackbirds. I didn't even see the Squirrels or *Stumpy* hang about for too long. A stunning young female Sparrowhawk landed on the top of the bird feeder. Mistress of all she surveyed, she sat there preening herself and looking around with those beady bright yellow eyes. She preened and watched; dropped to the floor for a minute to investigate, then returned to the perch. She was constantly alert, her head turning this way and that, the strong yellow talons on her bright yellow legs standing out almost symbolic of a latent threat. All was quiet. Nothing stirred. Then quickly and silently, she was off. Her flight was fast, powerful, and direct. She was gone and it was almost as if the Sparrowhawk had never been. Not that the baby Blue Tits saw it that way; everything laid low for quite some time; and you can hardly blame them.

Grey Squirrel. © Ian Rotherham

Wild about Ponds

Local botanist Steve Furness once said to me '*water equals life*'; and it is true. A large proportion of most living things *is* water; and it is also what ecologists describe as the 'fluid of life'. So if you want to attract wildlife to your site, be it a nature reserve or just your back garden, then a pond is a good idea. Of course with a garden pond or marsh you also have a great opportunity to bring colour, shade and light into the garden too. All the great landscape gardeners used water to create vistas and wonderful views. Water adds atmosphere and even timeliness to a landscape. Seasons are reflected in the colours around a pond, and the time of day makes a huge difference to light and reflection. I think ponds are also good for the soul; just try sitting and gazing into the depths!

Yellow-flowered Water Lily. © Ian Rotherham

Your garden pond brings all this and more. Okay it may bring the odd Mosquito as well, but that is a small price to pay for ecological richness and diversity; because that is what every pond, however large or small, gives you. I get plenty of messages about the anticipation and excitement of the first Frogs or Toads each year, and then of course there are all the Dragonflies too. I'm often asked about whether Goldfish are compatible with wildlife such as Newts and Frogs. The answer is a qualified yes. The ordinary Goldfish are not desperately predatory and if the pond is well designed with plenty of weed and also marshy fringes then there shouldn't be a problem. However, the more serious carnivores such as Orfes for example, may have a bad impact on your amphibians. But we also have the problem that a shallow pond full of brightly coloured Goldfish is heaven and an invite to lunch for birds like Grey Heron and Kingfisher. We then have a serious dilemma which is a bit like when the local Sparrowhawk starts dining off your tame Blue Tits. I've recently had a magnificent Grey Heron visiting nearby gardens and (I haven't told the Goldfish yet), but I feel chuffed to bits that it is coming down, and yes, to feed. Now my Brother-in-Law

Peter was really excited the other week. He is a very keen gardener and exceptionally proud of his achievements, including a beautiful garden pond full of Goldfish. Apparently he looked out of the house window and could see an unfamiliar greyish-looking bird hunched up on a rock by the pond. He could only see the back and it was in quite dark shade. This was a new visitor to the garden; but what was it? Well, once it flew up then it was obvious: a splendid adult Kingfisher. It moved around the pond for a while and dived in a few times, then eventually flew off. However, it must have been successful as it kept coming back for several days. Peter was so pleased, that he even put a branch sticking out of the ground to encourage it. I think he felt it was a real privilege to have such as brilliant bird visiting the garden and to have chance to view it at close quarters. I'm not sure his Goldfish will agree, but then nature is '*red in tooth and claw*' and the predators are some of our most spectacular wildlife. They also help the whole ecological cycle go around. It is difficult, and I realise that some people just find predators problematic; but that's life.

Whilst we're on the subject of water it is also the time of year that another quite rare predator comes out, the Grass Snake. Near canals, rivers or larger ponds then it is worth looking out for this (for us) harmless reptile. The females can be 3-4 feet long varying in colour from bright green to a dull green. Anywhere in the lowlands of our region then this is the most common snake; their range extending up river valleys certainly as far as Ecclesall and Norton in Sheffield. Watch out for these as they emerge from hibernation.

Thunderworms are go

I had letter and photograph from Stanley Wraith of Meersbrook, concerning something his daughter Sue and son-in-law Michael found in their garden. They live on Dobcroft Road in Millhouses, Sheffield. Their well-kept, tidy garden has a fair sized lawn, prone to flash flooding when it rains heavily. Of course this year has been particularly wet, and on the afternoon the water stood across the area. Now in some circumstances earthworms will emerge in wet weather. Quite often they are found dead and people think they've drowned. This is not the case as the worms can survive in water by 'breathing' through their moist skin. No, what happens is that in their burrows when the ground is waterlogged, the earthworms build up a high level of carbon dioxide (a waste product of breathing respiration), and come up to the surface to get a more oxygen-rich atmosphere. But on a sunny day, they are then killed by ultraviolet light in the intense sunshine.

Thunderworms © Stanley Wraith: winner of my *'Gross Wildlife of the Year'* Award for 2007

So earthworms at the surface would be a possibility, and the photograph Stanley sent is certainly of '*worms*', but not earthworms. They are a kind of roundworm or nematode, known as '*thunderworms*'. Summer showers will bring them out, and they may be up to around 20 cms (8 inches) in length, and described as a bit like brown cotton. They are mostly seen as they '*snake*' over wet plants and other materials on the ground, but will disappear back down below quite quickly once the water has gone. You may also find them during the summer if you pull plants up when weeding; they will be resting in amongst the plant roots. Thunderworms lay their eggs in the soil and then the young worms hatch, and a bit like the film '*Alien*' but on a micro-scale; they search out insects such as beetles, into which they burrow. Then, having fed on the tissues of their host animals, they grow into adults and depart to live in the soil. These animals are roundworms, and don't have the circular segments that earthworms clearly have. They are mostly parasitic on either animals or plants, and are some of the world's major pests for agriculture (for example the '*potato eelworm*'), and yes, for our pets too. These are the cousins of the roundworms that affect all our domestic pets. I suppose they are a component of

biodiversity, but a difficult one to campaign for. So it may be surprising and a bit disconcerting to know that they are probably the most abundant of all the planet's animals and there is almost nowhere on Earth from which they are absent. They are found in soil, in water, and in almost in and/or on every living plant or animal. Yuck! If that isn't enough it is suggested that if everything else living was swept away by a catastrophe that somehow left the nematodes, the outlines of the Earth, the mountains, the waters, and of all life, would still be visible etched out by the nematode worms. How about 20 million roundworms per square metre of soil surface, or 90,000 in one rotting apple; think about that next time you are scrumping apples or pears!

So Stanley's thunderworms probably lay about 600 eggs for each female, deposited in a tough bag or cyst. These are very resistant to dry weather and can remain viable in the soil for at least ten years. Now, down at '*Lower Dobby*', our brave, intrepid Sue managed to photograph these '*worms*' as they, very much alive and wriggling, squirmed over her lawn. They were in a mass of about 18 x 6 x 6 inches, and must take some sort of award for perhaps what my American friends would describe as '*Gross Wildlife of the Year*' Award for 2007. Congratulations and well done. Sue gets a copy of Mel Jones' *Sheffield's Woodland Heritage* book as a prize for Sue's bravery in the face of a large mass of wriggling thunderworms. I hope my description of what they are has set your minds at rest for next time they appear!

Garden Goldfinches and Moorland Hobbies

It was a couple of weeks ago driving close by Totley Moss; if you blinked, you missed it. An adult Hobby, the small cousin of the Peregrine Falcon flew fast and low over the road and onto the moor. I have seen them here before, and was once fortunate to have a family of two adult and their youngsters perched out on the millstone boulders. Not this time, but I suspect the family were nearby. The adults sport a dark cap with brilliant white cheeks, black moustache, the speckled underside is strongly marked, and the upper legs have strong russet red colours. With their sickle-like wings and fast flight, these are real show-offs! They chase the big dragonflies that favour the wet moorlands pools high above Totley, and feeding hungry youngsters keeps them busy.

Sheila Rimmington of Jenkin Road, Wincobank, emailed to say she had read and enjoyed my article about my garden. It was like a '*mirror image*' of hers (but no Woodpeckers). '*We only have a small garden and live at the top of Jenkin Road. We now get visits from wood pigeons and collared doves, which we never used to get a few years ago. The new visitor that we see, sometimes regularly and sometimes irregularly, is the sparrowhawk and I really do not like the idea of him / her feeding on 'my' birds especially the goldfinches which we don't have too many of! Over the time he has been visiting have actually witnessed him feeding about three times, the biggest catch being one of the collared doves.*' She asked, '*Are we making it easy for the predators by feeding the birds in our gardens?*', and attached a picture of the bird. The photograph shows a stunning male Sparrowhawk, with a blue-grey head and back and a white underside with rich orange stripes. If he is taking a collared dove then that is good going, and quite a big prey item. I wonder if there is a female coming in too. The female Sparrowhawk is brown in colour and much bigger than the male.

Hobby from a Victorian print

I think the answer to Sheila's question is '*yes*'. We attract many birds to feed regularly at garden feeders, so for a bird of prey it is a bit like an avian restaurant. The same goes for garden ponds and fish; and it is difficult to accept a Heron or Kingfisher taking your prize Goldfish. At the end of the day, nature is '*wild*' and not ethical or moral in any way, the birds of prey are wonderful creatures, but of course, they do have to eat! This is a bit troubling though when it is your Goldfinches or Blue Tits they are eating, or even a Collared Dove. I also suggested to Sheila that she tried the special Goldfinch feeders that dispense '*Thistle seed*', but she has already done that and got good results. (These actually dispense *Niger* seed not real Thistles). Goldfinches also love Teasel plants, one of my personal favourites for the wildlife garden. They should be in flower in the next week or so, and the butterflies and Bumblebees love them.

Fancy that

Small mammals like Shrews and Bats are highly active and also lose heat rapidly; a problem which increases the smaller size you are. To make up the loss they need to eat their own body-weight in insects, *etc* every day.

Grey Heron and Kingfishers are garden predators but welcomed by many

Grey Squirrels and Red Squirrels, and Red Grey Squirrels

Squirrel colouration is confusing. Back in the 1980s, Sorby Natural History Society undertook surveys of the different colour forms across the region, showing enormous variation. This variety causes much confusion and sightings of '*Red Squirrels*' are sent in when they are really '*red*' '*Grey Squirrels*'. Confused? It was about this phenomenon that Sid Wetherill of Raleigh Road wrote to me. He sent a close-up photograph of a squirrel that daily visits his garden, but looks neither red nor grey. It is a mottled grey and sandy brown, and is of course a Grey Squirrel. The undersides are white and the main areas that are reddish brown are around the eyes, along the flanks, and the sides of its legs. Now, to make things even more confusing, not all Red Squirrels are actually red! It was a fairly common practice in the early- to mid-1900s for landowners to import interesting animals from overseas to release in the UK, including unusual colour forms of animals such as Red Squirrel. Indeed, if any readers have been to parts of Germany where the native Red still does well, you may have noticed that they are not really red, but a dark russet and even totally black. These 'melanistic' forms were brought over and some released into local forestry estates such as Chatsworth. This used to cause endless confusion when Grey Squirrels were still rare and Reds were common, plus all the colours in between. We still get records of 'Red Squirrels', but nowadays these unfortunately are all like Sid's Squirrels in his garden, a Grey Squirrel with red bits. Our native Reds have certainly gone; the observation sent to me by John Gilvarry from Bamford Golf Course in 1984, being a very late record. I have a few more after his date, but not many. I did even try to get a campaign going to save our local and regional Red Squirrels, but the '*the powers that be*' could not really see the point. This is a pity really, when there are now some excellent projects around the UK to safeguard and celebrate this most iconic of our mammals. It seems sad to me that a child growing up in South Yorkshire or North Derbyshire will never see one, unless they are on holiday (the child, not the squirrels!)

If you do want to see a Red Squirrel in the wild then the best place is *Ainsdale Dunes National Nature Reserve*, nears Sefton on the east coast of Lancashire. Check out the web site and head for the car park at the south of the Nature Reserve. Not only Red Squirrels literally performing for you, but loads of other wildlife too. It is a great wild day out and not too far to go. You could take in *Martin Mere Wildfowl and Wetlands Trust Centre* on the way back, and the facilities there are great with access for the less

able, lots of kids stuff, and a nice restaurant and shops. Full details are on the Wildfowl and Wetlands Trust web site.

Finally, I am conducting a little experiment and want to hear of readers' ideas or experiences. I have a problem with Squirrels carting off bucket-loads of peanuts before my garden birds get a chance to eat them Now, having bought squirrel-proof nut holders, the blighters are at my fat balls! My neighbour Mike has suggested sprinkling the nuts and the fat balls with cayenne pepper. Apparently, the birds cannot taste it, and it does no harm to either Squirrels or birds. However, does it work? Have you any experience of this or any other suggestions? I can see me working up to curried nuts with fat balls in a light pepper sauce. It seems to discourage the Squirrels taking the nuts, but they have moved on to fat balls with a vengeance.

There's buzz in the air!

Marjoram: one of the best insect plants.© Ian Rotherham

It is all very exciting. In recent years, the good old Honey Bee has had a bad time. Last year I didn't see a single one in my garden at Norton. So imagine my surprise and delight when they turned up in abundance this summer. These were the bees of my childhood, lately almost wiped out by a nasty disease carried by a parasitic mite. Almost all the wild Honey Bees and many domesticated ones were killed. Bumblebees on the other hand have done rather well in our gardens, and a recent report (a paper in the

Journal of Applied Ecology) highlighted that this is now the most important habitat for Bumblebees. So much so, that bumblebee numbers have increased in gardens as money bees have dropped off. It is not all good news though. There are twenty-five native species of Bumblebees and three are nationally extinct with fifteen others in decline. Sadly, much of the decline is due to modern, intensive agricultural methods. We've lost the old hay meadows and pastures and the bits of rough ground. These are the places where the bees nest and forage. Old lanes with hedgerows and grassy verges are good bee habitat, with up to thirty bumblebee nests per hectare (which is about half a football pitch). They need the rich wildflowers and their nectar, and then rough ground and more dense vegetation for the nests. You can help the Bumblebees in your garden by leaving some rough areas a bit unkempt. It is best to locate a bee area somewhere sunny, and where they won't be disturbed. A few upturned, broken plant pots and maybe a little rubble will also help encourage them. Then just stand back and wait for nature to take its course. Also, there's absolutely no need to worry about getting stung. A Bumblebee will sting, but only in extreme circumstances. Unlike Hive Bees or wasps, around the nest they are very placid. The big bees are the fertile females, and the nests have numbers of smaller worker bees. You can safely stand by the nest and watch the activities of the workers coming and going with their pollen sacs full. Of course they are also doing a hugely important job in pollinating all the garden and agricultural plants too.

This is one reason why farmers and horticultural growers such as fruit farms and orchards, were so worried about the decline of the Honey Bee. They are very important to the economy. No bees = no fruit. That is a serious problem. In the case of the Honey Bee, it is likely that they too have suffered with the way the environment has been damaged over the last fifty years or so. However, the immediate problem is a disease over which we probably have very little control. For the bumblebees in the wider countryside, as is often the case, the problem is largely self-inflicted by people. We simply don't seem to learn from our mistakes, or perhaps we just don't care enough; although the price we pay is high.

Well you can do your bit to help, and it is really quite easy. This won't solve the bigger problem, but surely every little step in the right direction is worthwhile? Leaving some rough, sunny parts of the garden undisturbed helps, but what bees like is nectar and pollen. They love flowers! So the next step is to plant all sorts of good old fashioned herbs and cottage garden plants; good rich sources of nectar and pollen. I have loads of marjoram in flower at the moment and the bees are all over it. It self-seeds and there are two good varieties, one with the standard green foliage and the other a golden variety with lovely golden-yellow leaves. Other things to plant include Lavender and all the varieties of Thyme. The aim is to have flowers out and available at all times of day, and as sunny as possible, and throughout as much of the year as you can. You will really enjoy it, literally getting a buzz in your garden, and you'll be helping nature as well.

Fancy that

One of our first spring flowers is the tiny Lesser Celandine. It is also known as '*Pilewort*', since in herbal medicine it was used to treat piles, apparently with some success. Let me know if you've tried it.

Bumblebees. © Stanley Wraith

I had a message from local naturalist Austin Brackenbury about bees. He pointed out that the reappearance of my Honey Bees could well be due to a local bee keeper keeping their hives nearby. I agree and think that is likely. The bees themselves look like a domesticated hive bees rather than wild bees, although it is difficult to be sure. Interestingly, as I said and Austin agrees, the wild Honey Bee is now very rare. He saw his last ones in a hollow tree in Oakes Park, close to where I live. This was in the mid-1990s, and around that time our department at Hallam University was moving from the campus at Totley Hall. I remember that a south-facing wall in one of the 1950s brick buildings had a massive swarm of Honey Bees. They really were everywhere. That was before the diseases kicked in and the populations were decimated. Unfortunately the problems affect both wild bees and those with beekeepers. Perhaps it helps if we all do our bit to provide lots of nectar-rich and pollen-rich flowers in our gardens; maybe.

Pheasants in the Garden

One of our most striking birds is the Common or Eurasian Pheasant. Not a native, it was brought from eastern areas to Europe by the Greeks, and then by the Romans to Britain. So I can confidently ask '*What did the Romans do for us?*' and the answer would be they introduced the Pheasant. However, it isn't clear whether their birds actually established in the wild; what we would call a '*feral*' population. As with quite a few species (such as Brown Hare and Fallow Deer for example), it was left to the Normans to reintroduce when Roman stock had perished. Indeed William '*The Bastard*' (I kid you not!) dined on roast Pheasant just before the Battle of Hastings; after which he of course rose through the ranks to become William the Conqueror.

Anyway, a couple of weeks ago I mentioned unusual sightings of Pheasants around the region and this sparked a number of responses. Jan Peel from Wadsley wrote: '*I was fascinated to hear about pheasants in your column. About ten years ago I saw a cock pheasant stroll across the lawn one tea time. I grabbed my camera and crept out to take a picture of him but he was nowhere to be seen. I ended up looking under every bush in the garden as I was sure he was still there but couldn't believe something so colourful could hide in what was then a very bare winter garden. I gave up and as soon as I sat down indoors he strolled back across the lawn, head held high. We called him George, and could sometimes see his very shy partner, Mavis, scuttling about in the woods behind our house but she never came in the garden. Ten years later George, or probably son of George, spends most of his day in our garden with no less than three daughters of Mavis. He used to march crossly away if we dared to venture out into 'his' garden, but now he doesn't bother. He has even gone into the duck run several times when my husband feeds them. Even the Mavises (Maevi?) have given up doing a disconcerting vertical take off if we happen to walk past a bush they are under. George stays just beyond arms reach but even Mavis stayed quite close the other day. I started to prune a bamboo and there she was sitting underneath. She just moved a few feet away and looked dolefully back at me. As I write, George is in his customary place under the bird feeder, waiting for the smaller birds to drop seeds. He looks so handsome and proud, looking round while Mavis pecks at his feet. I could admire his plumage all day, and I'm sure I'm not the only one as I saw Mavis display to him last week. Her tail spread in an arc like a fan. Wonderful! What a privilege to be part of their lives.*'

Jan goes on to note that both George and one Mavis are rather large birds, in fact they are huge and round but its the other busy birds who feed them, dropping seed. They get a bit of grain from the ducks as well. They also boast a big fan club amongst Jan's neighbours. So they are both plump and popular. She also asks about unusual plumaged Pheasants, apparently very dark, either black or blue-purple, depending on the light, around the Damflask area. This variation in colour isn't too unusual as many Pheasants are bred and released; so coloured forms may be deliberately introduced. I'll come on to this in more detail in a couple of weeks. In the meantime has anybody else seen odd coloured Pheasants here, or indeed elsewhere? Let me know.

Birds, Birds, Birds….!

Pheasants are still causing a stir across the region. Simon Robinson of Stannington wrote concerning recent correspondence on pheasants. A friend showed him *On The Wild Side* and this struck a chord. *'We recently began seeing pheasants in our Stannington garden. We're lucky to live near fields so were used to seeing them after moving here ten years ago. However, during late 2006, a male started trotting up the road in the early morning investigating the gardens, and finding bird-seed on the ground, coming right up to the house. Soon he, another male and two females, were visiting daily,*

Little Grebe now widespread on our rivers, reservoirs and ponds. © Ian Rotherham

sometimes spending most of the day in the back garden. They were nervous at first but now see us as the intruders. As we garden for wildlife (our latest treat has been a weasel hopping across our vegetable patch, and a less welcome rogue mole!), we're pleased to see them. I'm not sure about our neighbours' opinions as the birds have become bolder and venture into other gardens. Currently the females have been absent for around ten days, so we think they are sitting on eggs at a nearby field margin. Working from home, we have delivery drivers, and one in particular always has to see the pheasant. He said that he has noticed quite an increase in this area on his rounds over the last eighteen months. Perhaps this is due to the milder winters of late. I did photograph one of the males during the last fall of snow we had in February; very picturesque.'

James Young photographed the black Pheasant shown below, but up in North Yorkshire. What a stunning bird.

Black Pheasant. © James Young

It does seem that the numbers are increasing and that Pheasants are coming more and more into gardens. Michael Parker of Deepcar wrote: *'As I accompanied my mate Andy on a walk around the Ewden Valley on Saturday (April 21st) we saw what we took to be a male pheasant that was completely black in colour wandering about the field at the bottom of New Mill Bank. Incidentally it was in close to two normally-coloured cock pheasants and a female. We thought this was quite odd as we'd never seen a 'black' pheasant before. So we put it down to some sort of genetic anomaly on a par with an albino blackbird for example. Indeed, in recent weeks a blackbird with white patches on its upper wing surface has visited my garden regularly. However, a little while later, around noon, we were walking along Storth Lane to Brightholmlee. Here we spied another large bird running down the lane in front of us. As it turned side-on to us, to dart through a gap in the hedge, we could clearly see that it was once again a more plump, black, cock pheasant but this time with long white tail-feathers. Well one sighting we thought rather unusual, but two on the same day within an hour or so of each other in separate locations with differently coloured tail feathers?! We would be grateful if you could provide us with a possible explanation.'* Michael also saw a house martin, which in April is a reasonably early record.

Garden Pheasant. © Simon Robinson

There is certainly an increase in pheasant numbers and especially in oddly-coloured ones. At Chatsworth where I do a regular river-bird survey, there are lots of dark purple/almost black coloured male Pheasants, and both pale and dark form females. Colour-forms or morphs are linked to a single or simple group of genes. So it is like a black (melanistic) Mallard, a white (albino) Blackbird, or the less common buff (leucistic)

bird, for example a Lapwing. The oddest-looking bird I've seen was an albino crow out on Totley Moss a couple of years ago. That looked very strange indeed! Let me know what you've seen, and I'll find out more about the black Pheasants.

Desirable Residence Suitable for Blue Tits; Enquire within

I had a letter from Alan Lowis of Maplebeck Drive about Blue Tits and nest-boxes; this struck a chord. He has a nest-box on his garage; its location just the same as his neighbour's; but there's a difference. Alan's nest-box is ignored whilst his neighbour's is a rip-roaring success! The neighbour's box has nesting Blue Tits every year for the past ten years and sometimes two broods. To rub salt in the wound, during the early spring of each year, the Blue Tits prospect around and inspect Alan's box. They then, having tantalised Alan and his wife with the prospect of success, disappear until the same time next year. Life is cruel. I'm not sure what the solution is or even what is happening. If it is any comfort to know, I have exactly the same problem. I've put up several boxes around the garden in what to me seem to be ideal locations; on quite big trees, shaded from sun and sheltered from wind and rain. The holes are perfect, they are luxurious and I've even thought about rigging up Sky TV for them. But no luck! Alan says he's considering lowering the rent; well maybe. I suspect there may be something that the birds simply prefer about next door. It may also be that if there is more than one pair on Blue Tits, then the ones next door are seeing off Alan's; the birds are highly territorial and won't tolerate a close neighbour. (People can be quite similar!). It is incredibly frustrating and as he says both he and his wife get enormous pleasure from watching a whole variety of birds in the garden. The nesting Blue Tits would really crown it. He could perhaps move the box, maybe as far from the neighbour's box as possible. Beyond that a sign saying *'Desirable Blue Tit Residence this way…'* I wonder if anyone else has had this problem… or better still, solved it.

Congratulations to Margaret and Roger Mosforth of Crawshaw Avenue for sending a record and picture of Variegated Yellow Archangel from Park Bank Wood, Beauchief. They win copies of Mel Jones' *Sheffield's*

Woodland Heritage, and Julie Bunting's *Bygone Industries of the Peak*. So thanks for the record of this plant now showing well and spreading rapidly across our region! More records please; any over to the east in Doncaster, Rotherham or Barnsley?

Variegated Yellow Archangel flowering in April sent in © Margaret and Roger Mosforth

But back to the garden birds and how Blue Tits and Great Tits are very competitive and territorial; and for good reason. The territory of each breeding pair must supply and feed the adults whilst nesting and incubating, and then the entire brood once fledged. There's no room for sentiment or for neighbours. I recall seeing a pair of Great Tits with recently fledged young in a tree by a Derbyshire Dales riverside. Close by a family of around eight baby Blue Tits sat on a branch attended by their parents; all really pretty and rather delightful. Then, one by one, the Great Tits picked off each baby Blue Tit, flew off with them to a nearby branch, repeatedly pecking with their beaks. They then carried the now limp babies and dropped them a considerable distance to the ground. Children nearby were very distressed, and parents struggled to explain what

was happening. I suppose it is all down to the old cliché of '*nature red in tooth and claw*'. We sometimes forget that wildlife is really '*wild*'; it has no moral values and makes no judgements; it just survives. For the Great Tits, the family of Blue Tits was a threat to their survival; with both sets of young fledged and so close together the situation was obviously acute. They resolved it the only way they could.

On the Derbyshire Derwent I saw a similar interaction quite recently. As far I know this didn't end in fatality, although if youngsters were around who knows? A pair of Coots near to Chatsworth House Bridge was defending its territory very zealously. I'd noticed them previously and they were aggressive, even to me; calling loudly and throwing themselves backwards into the water, splashing with their wings. This time they were in dispute with a pair of Moorhens; obviously direct competition for space. First of all it was one Coot against two Moorhens; the latter putting up a pretty good defence of their patch. However, after a few minutes the second of the Coots arrived and chased the Moorhens up into the lower branches of an overhanging tree, and there lost to sight. I wonder what happened next.

The Eagle has landed!?

Well not an Eagle but pretty close; Steve Smith emailed a note and a picture: '*I was out waiting for a train to pass at Treeton back in October 2006 but while I was by the iron bridge, a large bird landed, eating something like a mouse. I've shown this picture to my friend who believes it is a Red Kite. To me it looks more like an Eagle. Please can you tell me what I saw?*' Steve and his friend are not far off, and I see why both came up with their identifications. The bird is a North American Harris Hawk – equivalent to our Common Buzzard. They are kept over here by falconers and do escape; often showing falconer's leather jesses attached to their legs, but not always. Wow, what a sight, what a picture! Another identification clue is the bird's behaviour. Our native wild raptors (birds of prey) of this size would not let you get so close so easily. It may have been eating a Mouse, a Vole, or even a young Rabbit, or a Brown Rat. There was a Harris Hawk around Tinsley/Blackburn Meadows Nature Reserve for a few years.

Treeton isn't far away and these birds are long-lived. Perhaps it is the same one? I wonder if anybody else has seen this.

Harris Hawk. © Steve Smith

To the west of our area Graham Shepherd emailed an interesting sighting, but one that will remain tantalisingly unidentifiable! His message was '*Hi Ian, I was very interested in your recent Buzzard reports in The Star. Two weeks ago in Little Matlock Woods (west Sheffield) I disturbed a bird very similar to the Buzzard shown in the picture. It was substantially larger than a Sparrowhawk and when it flew I could see on its top side, a distinct white band about an inch wide at the base of each wing. I was wondering if this helps identify it.*' Well, as often the case with birds of prey, this is difficult to say. Also, and to complicate things, round there you could get any of the local birds of prey, plus escapes like Steve's bird. Goshawk, a big female Sparrowhawk, or Common Buzzard are all possible. I asked Graham if he had any more detail but there was nothing he could remember. The sort of things I would be looking for are how it flew, tail shape, wing shape (length / breadth, pointed or rounded). All these are useful clues. My feeling with Graham's bird is that he could well be right, and it may have been a Buzzard. They are very variable in plumage and can have quite a lot of white on the wings. However, they are often a bit '*blotchy*' rather than a band of white; so I'm not totally convinced. If the view was of the underside,

then Common Buzzard does show a white trailing edge. Anyway, for birdwatchers this is the type of record that is the equivalent of the fisherman's '*one that got away*'. It is best to accept (reluctantly) that the bird remains enigmatic, than force it into something we're not sure of. The temptation is always to try to be '*sure*' of what is was. Sometimes, and this is one of those, we can't be. These records can generate hours of speculation over a pint or two in the pub trying to work out if it was this, that or the other. Regionally records are sent in to recording bodies such as the *Sheffield Bird Study Group* (or SBSG for those in the know). They go through a very rigorous vetting process before being accepted or rejected. Believe it or not, our Victorian predecessors used to shoot the birds they recorded and so provide a skin as proof of evidence! In fact a local man and nationally eminent and pioneering ornithologist, Charles Dixon of Meersbrook in Sheffield, was one of the first people to advocate watching through opera glasses and not shooting on site. Incidentally, if you are keen on birds and not an SBSG member, then do join. It is very friendly, very informative and great value. Let me know if you need details of this or other groups across the region.

Booming Birdlife

Despite conservation attempts the state of some bird species in Britain is pretty dire. Some of the declines of farmland birds have been halted and the Tree Sparrow for example now seems to be increasing. Others like the Turtle Dove still seem to be nose-diving. This is a real shame as they were one of the special birds of the Moss Valley or areas like Wentworth. Alas no more. But some birds are on the up, either through conservation measures or simply the way the environment is changing. Many species are closely dependent on climate and we lose some and gain others. Some increases such as for the Little Egret, a small white heron, have been spectacular. We don't see them up here yet, but we undoubtedly will in decades to come. In the last few years, we have seen the Crane back as a breeding bird in East Anglia, and the Spoonbill, another former breeder in extensive wetlands, is returning. The Marsh Harrier has picked up from a handful of pairs in the 1980s, to a thriving population, including in our region. Red Kites too have returned, though with a big helping hand through reintroduction programmes; head up to Harewood Hall near Wetherby if you fancy spectacular views of these magnificent birds.

We also have pleasing increases in birds such as Raven, Peregrine Falcon, and of course Buzzard back in our region. These bigger birds of prey are always especially vulnerable to illegal persecution as well as accidental disturbance. Some of the smaller birds have also done well, so Long-tailed Tit and Goldfinch now seem more abundant than they once were. Of course all the wildlife gardeners and a series of mild winters have helped a lot of smaller birds survive. It is good to know that we are all doing our bit to help.

Raven making a welcome return

There has also been an increase in the sightings of very rare birds; what are often called vagrants. These are generally species that shouldn't really be here but perhaps get blown off course by bad weather and end up on the wrong continent. For serious bird-watchers this is big news. In the old days you relied on luck to find such birds, and then if you were '*in the know*', on the '*grapevine*'. This could of course lead to frustration and bitterness if people felt they were left out and missed a new bird of a '*lifer*'. Bird-watching can get very competitive. However, all this has changed with the advent of new technology. Network and information exchange have become easier and faster. Records are co-ordinated by a range of organisations, but a lot of information is available through BirdGuides.com; which of course originated in Sheffield. In 2007, there

was a bumper crop of 'mega-rarities' such as Long-billed Murrelet in Devon, Yellow-nosed Albatross in Somerset (and closer to home for us in Lincolnshire too), and Masked Booby on the south coast off Portland in Dorset. There have also been Great Blue Herons from North America and Great White Egrets from Europe. Nowadays there is much more sophisticated networking and monitoring, so more new birds are found. Unusual and extreme weather can mean good numbers of rare birds off their usual track. Sadly of course many of these won't survive. They are out of their normal range and in foreign habitat. Many will be stressed and exhausted after a long and perilous journey. I recall a debate over one rare bird (I think it was in the Scillies), which died during a mega bird-watch. Having travelled considerable distances, and often at great expense, there were heated debates about exactly at what point of the bird's death could a record still stand. These were rather morbid but serious issues for some of the twitchers. If it was still warm did it count as a successful tick?

It is also worth remembering that our wild bird populations are by no means static. A now familiar and common bird like the Collared Dove is a relative newcomer and arrived under its own steam. Others like the Little Owl or '*Frenchie*' were deliberately introduced; in this case, by enthusiasts about 100 years ago, surviving extermination campaigns in the 1930s. At the moment Little Egret, followed by Cattle Egret and perhaps even Great White Egret, all members of the Heron Family, may be becoming established in Britain.

The South Yorkshire Buffaloes

Michael Parker asks about one of our region's most unusual '*wildlife*' records, the herd of American Buffalo at Wharncliffe Chase. These beasts were kept in the imparked area of the Chase, along with the more conventional herd of Red Deer. Michael's enquiry follows from my recent article about exotic species introduction. In my research on old parks, I have come across other records of Buffalo. These were the North American cousins of the rather rare, European Bison, and are most correctly called Bison. This helps to distinguish them from the Water Buffalo which produce Buffalo Mozzarella cheese, and are used increasingly for grazing in nature reserve management. These Water Buffalo come in two main types, a wild and potentially very dangerous one that you will see in Africa (and on wildlife documentaries), and a domesticated (or semi-domesticated) Oxen. The latter are found in Southern Europe, Africa, and Asia. The letter from Michael notes that Henry Tatton's notebook states that '*As a boy, when at Wharncliffe Lodge, I was taken to a wall opposite and lifted up to see the buffaloes in the Park. Their heads and pelts are preserved at Wortley Hall, the seat of the Earl of Wharncliffe.*' John Holland in 1861 went further when he described Wharncliffe Chase as '*A tract of old forest, scattered over with oaks that have evidently weathered centuries of storms; bulky, bossy, stag-headed, and gray, they harmonize admirably with the deer and bisons that range the chase.*' There are even accounts in local newspapers of the escape of four buffaloes, two apparently brown in colour and the others described as white, (which seems unusual to me). These were said to have escaped from the Earl Fitzwilliam's estate at Wentworth Park (i.e. Wentworth Woodhouse, where there is again a herd of deer), in December 1881. Three of these were recaptured quite quickly, but one made off for Swinton Junction. Here, perhaps annoyed at a cancelled train, (I know how it felt), it charged and head-butted a stationary steam locomotive. Not surprisingly, it collapsed stunned and exhausted. Unfortunately, it was then '*despatched*' by a railway official with a hammer; oh for British Rail! I presume that the locals in Swinton dined well for a few weeks. A picture passed to me by Mel Jones entitled '*Scotch Bullocks and Buffaloes, Wentworth Woodhouse*' remains a bit of a mystery as the Highland Cattle (Scotch Bullocks) are shown very clearly, but there's nothing which looks remotely like a Buffalo. Some pale cattle in the picture even look a little like old-fashioned Longhorns.

A Bison or North American '*Buffalo*' from a Victorian print

Michael would like to know more about these exotics in our region, and so would I. How many were there, when did they arrive, and when were the last ones '*despatched*'? It was suggested that the preserved heads *etc* were kept at Wortley Hall, but according to Michael, a search there has revealed nothing. However, the Wharncliffe Estate ran into serious and well-publicised problems with the last resident Earl. The main belongings were I believe either sold, or removed to the nearby Wharncliffe House, and I do remember once going there in the 1990s, and rooms were packed with all sorts of items from the old Hall. Maybe that's where they went. I also know that the leather bound '*Game Book*s' that recorded the game animals and birds in the Chase, went missing from the Estate Office about the same time. This is a real shame since it could shed more light on the enigma of the South Yorkshire Buffalo. If anybody knows of their whereabouts then please let me know.

I'm sure that somewhere I have a photograph of one of the Buffaloes, but I just cannot find it. If anyone out there can let me have more information, or even photographs, that would be great. Does anybody know of other individuals or herds across the region? This might be one for my friend Professor Melvyn Jones, the Radio Sheffield History Man, to answer! It was certainly not that unusual for the great landowners to have extensive collections or menageries; often in cages or glasshouses, but larger beats out in the park. A body known as the *Acclimatisation Society* actively promoted such ideas during the mid-1800s. This body was co-ordinated by Victorian zoologist Frank Buckland. He felt that the American Bison (along with many other species) might be advantageously acclimatised in Britain, and carrying its hump on its shoulders, its taste appeal to *gourmets*. Well it has taken nearly 200 years but you can now get local buffalo steaks and sausages, and they are a healthy option to beef!

Would you Adam and Eve it?

Ancient trees are some of our most evocative and iconic features in the landscape. If they occur in your local patch, or perhaps a favourite place to visit, then they really make the place special. The impact even goes beyond the life of the tree itself. An ancient Oak for example, can stand for many decades, possible a century even, after death. Of course from an ecological viewpoint, the tree itself is dead, but it still provides a resource that is rich in life. Fungi, mosses, lichens, rare beetles and flies, and birds like woodpeckers and Treecreepers continue to use the venerable Oak skeleton long after the spirit of the tree has gone (as Monty Python would say) to '*meet its maker*'. This can mean that in some situations we remove '*dead*' trees before we perhaps should. In doing this we can, often unwittingly, erase a unique and unfortunately irreplaceable part of our heritage. Trees that are our veterans now, maybe 350 years or more old, even up to 1,000 years plus, are what we increasingly call '*working trees*'. This basically means that in time past, and often until relatively recently, in some cases up to the 1950s, they literally worked for their living. These trees were carefully tended to produce wood for fuel, timber for buildings, bark for tanning, acorns and Beech mast for your pigs, and leaf fodder for livestock. Before the advent of DIY stores, electricity and gas on tap *etc*, such products were vital to survival. They still are in some parts of the world. In many cases the tree management was a '*cut and come again*' system, that was inherently sustainable. The great trees that we have inherited often result from this use over centuries, and now those uses have almost all ceased. So when we lose these trees they cannot be replaced, even over a long time, because the system that produced them has stopped. In some cases there were particular uses, and special skills needed, that we don't even know about. When you view such a veteran or have chance to get in close and touch one,

you really are connecting with times past and the lives and work of those woodmen and country people who depended on this valuable resource. Then as now, the trees and the woods were a source of conflict and of discontent, between owners and other local people who might wish to stake a claim, or make use of the products. Mel Jones has a wonderful series of posters from the Duke of Norfolk warning '*All Nutters*' to keep out of his Grace's woodlands; they were of course after his hazelnuts.

Eve still standing at Unstone near Dronfield. © Ian Rotherham

So with all this said, I was pleased to see a wonderful old veteran still in good hands at Unstone, in the field just opposite Unstone Grange. This is one of two great Oaks called Adam and Eve. Adam fell over in 1929, and was still lying in pieces behind the farmhouse in the early 1950s. Apparently they are immortalised on a postcard from the early 1920s, showing the *Twin Oaks of Unstone*, and also by an oil painting from the 1800s. I was fortunate to meet the local farmer of (I presume) Grange Farm, and who was very knowledgeable about the trees. I remembered being shown Eve (still standing), back in about 1975, so it is reassuring to see her still their and in good and caring hands. There is even a Millennium Oak planted alongside for the future; again a nice touch. An old saying is that an oak grows for 300 years, lives for 300 years, and gracefully declines for 300 years; and Oliver Rackham states that an ancient oak is worth 10,000 planted trees. Eve's been biologically dead for decades, but will stand for many more. When she falls, left alone she will still be there long after we have passed on; which makes you think. If anybody has pictures of the Twin Oaks of Unstone, or of similar images of the region's veteran trees or indeed any stories surrounding them, I'd love to know.

In the Bleak Midwinter

If you spotted any Reindeer over Christmas then my researcher Martin Derbyshire would like your records for his regional Deer Survey! Just send them into me c/o 'On the Wild Side', the *Sheffield Star*. Incidentally the rutting season for the Red Deer is over but you might hear Roe or Muntjac barking in the late evening; let us know. We did have queries about safety and the wild Red Deer on the moors west of Sheffield.

My advice was that Red Deer were very safe and will avoid you, but as a large mammal, the male with big antlers, then *'respect is due'*!! However, I have an update. A number of correspondents have mentioned the rutting stags appearing to take *'an interest in them'* and even *'follow them down the path'*. OK, so a footnote to my advice and especially for the fairer sex. Red Deer stags when rutting may take an interest in female pheromones … so you've been warned for next year!

Janet Oliver emailed to ask about bats around Wentworth Woodhouse. She says an article in *The Star* a few months ago, maybe in July, caught her interest. It was about rare bats living at Wentworth but she is struggling to find out much more. She would like to know as her Granddaughter is studying bats and she would be most interested. So if anyone can let me have more information on bats in that area, then I'll pass it on. Wentworth is certainly an excellent area for bats, and around the great house and the lakes there will be both the Pipistrelle species, Brown Long-eared, Daubenton's, Noctule, and perhaps the rare Leisler's. There may be others but I don't have the information and didn't see the article. However, this is a classic situation where there are groups out there who would love to help. If you want good information for this sort of thing then I would try the web site of the *Sorby Natural History Society* and check out their reports/books on local mammals. Their publications are listed on the site and are generally cheap perhaps costing *c*. £5 for a copy and well worth a read. If you can't find them, let me know and I'll get you the details. For an enquiry like this I'd also suggest you try on Google *'Barnsley Biodiversity Action Plan'* + *'bats'* (try Rotherham too, but I'm not sure how much you'll find) and also the *National Biodiversity Network* web site should help too. You might try the web site of the *Yorkshire Wildlife Trust* as well; and in Derbyshire, Nottinghamshire or Lincolnshire, the appropriate county trust. A lot of these won't give specific site details; either for conservation reasons or simply because they haven't got them. This is again where you can help by just getting involved and recording – most groups would love to train you up! They also often need support in basic things like administration, fund-raising, and IT work. So, no excuses just get out there and do your bit.

Making a comeback, the Bittern from a Victorian print

There's been an interesting sighting around Rother Valley with a Bittern in the lakes of the country park land earmarked to become the new *YES Centre*. Let's hope the developers take this wonderful wildlife into account. The Bitterns are back in numbers as wintering birds at the fantastic Potteric Carr Yorkshire Wildlife Trust Nature Reserve near Doncaster. They are showing well, so if you fancy a post-Christmas walk with good bird-watching and there's a cold snap then it is ideal for Bitterns and the otherwise elusive Water Rail too. Also, the Meersbrook Parakeet is still around so watch out. In times past the people of the fens used to eat Bittern and as a dish it compared favourably with young Herons. Both, as might be expected, were a bit fishy.

A Little Bit of Christmas Cheer

The weather is certainly affecting local wildlife. Wild and garden plants simply haven't worked out it really is winter; I've lots of Ox-eye Daisies, Fuchsias, and even Roses in bloom. Not much '*snow lying round about, deep and crisp and even*'! This week a few garden birds have perked up their appetites with more species and greater numbers on the

birdfeeders: Nuthatch, Great Spotted Woodpecker, Blue Tit, Great Tit, and Goldfinches. A few cold nights are bringing them in, but it still doesn't have that Christmas feel. A Blue Tit checked out one of my nest-boxes, and a pair of Dunnocks displayed and perhaps more but they disappeared behind a bush!! Kirsty Swinburn at Charnock says she's heard Mistle Thrush singing; is it a sign of early breeding? It might be, but not necessarily. Mistle Thrushes like Blackbirds are territorial in the breeding season. However, they get decidedly stroppy around favourite berry bushes or fruit trees in winter, displaying and repelling rival Thrushes, Blackbirds and Fieldfares. Mistle Thrushes or Mistletoe Thrushes bring me to Christmas. Many of our oldest and most cherished Christmas customs are neither so traditional (in some cases), or '*Christmasy*' (in others), as we might think. Most of the cults of greenery such as Holly, Mistletoe, and in some regions Rosemary, Bay or other evergreens are decidedly pagan; with fertility and sexual overtones.

Mistletoe from a Victorian print

So what about '*Father Christmas*' a man of many aliases like St Nicholas and Santa Claus? Well he didn't celebrate Christmas and knew little about Reindeer. In Dutch legends

'Sinterklaas' rides a grey horse, wearing bishop's clothes (well I suppose it takes all sorts at Christmas ……). If you head north you may come across the Finnish legend of '*Old Man Winter*' who does drive his reindeer down from the mountains and brings the snow with him. So we now have a man who sounds like he sports a long white beard and is involved with Reindeer. The image of Santa that we see everywhere - as the plump, jolly figure, long white beard *etc* is depressingly recent. It comes from the drawings of Thomas Nast in *Harpers Weekly* between 1863 and 1886; the fur-trimmed robe inspired by the furs of the wealthy Astors. However, there is worse to come (**SO SMALL OR SENSITIVE CHILDREN SHOULD NOT READ BEYOND THIS POINT**). Our 'traditional' Santa in shops, in gardens, in corporate displays, on cards, inflated and illuminated in countless balconies of homes in for example the Gleadless Valley across to Dinnington, and from Askern to Grimethorpe, is a complete fraud, a charlatan. The jovial bundle of fun and merriment clad in red and white (a Blades fan of course!), is the invention of Coca-Cola. Before 1931, Santa Claus had different garbs from a natty green elf number, to a sombre St. Nicholas; in one he was a gaunt man in animal skins or straw, called Knecht Rupprecht, and apparently rather frightening. English legends relate to the '*Green Man*'; not '*Swampy*' or David Bellamy but an image harking back to pagan ancestors, the spirit of nature and the wildwood. From our Viking ancestors was the Norse god Odin in the depths of winter visiting his worshippers with gifts for the deserving and punishments the bad; a few folk should be looking out around Yuletide! In some pictures I have of him, Santa looks anything from just plain glum to downright evil and scary. He clearly had a good PR assistant in the 1900s and his brand was re-launched.

Anyway Coca-Cola commissioned young Swedish artist, Haddon Sundblom to do an image makeover; in modern parlance a bit of spin. It worked a treat with St. Nicholas wearing a red coat with white trim and a thick leather belt, and posed various seasonal scenes. In 1934, he gained a hat also trimmed in white. He also lost his pipe and gained a bottle of Coke (the drink and not as far as I know the white

powder); posing with children, reindeer, sacks of toys, or letters. His very modest gifts of things such as cakes, fruit, nuts, dolls and items of clothing, also became much more expensive and led to the pinnacle of the consumer-driven Christmas experience. This really is the American dream! But what was he smoking in that pipe? Just ordinary tobacco; I don't think so. Anyway, have a '*Cool Yule and a Happy Hogmanay*'; just one thought: '*Don't forget, environmental catastrophe isn't just for Christmas, with any luck there'll be a bit left over for Boxing Day*!'

Merry Christmas from St Nikolaas; and I think he looks a little bit evil!

Enjoying a Wild Christmas

I'm sure everyone will have lots of Christmas cards with pictures of Robins; the good old English Redbreast; as symbolic of good old Anglo-Saxon roots as roast beef and of course roast turkey. Well perhaps not Turkey as that is a recent important from our (former) American colonies. In times past you'd more likely sit down to roast goose or perhaps if of a sufficiently high standing, roast Swan. The poor would be lucky to be getting much at all; and were probably very grateful even for a few scraps. The other complication and big difference between say now and the Middle Ages would be your basic comfort zone. First of all there was no double glazing and no central heating. Many people simply died of cold because of a lack of fuel, and others starved. To top it all, of course it was cold, and I mean really *COLD*. Historians used to call the 'Little Ice Age'; so not a bit *'parky'* but really bitterly cold. In parts of Scotland for example there were periods when the temperature did not rise above freezing for over two years. Now it only *feels* like that. By Victorian times the middle classes and business classes were emerging in urban centres, and with coal fires we got heat but dreadful pollution. However, this did shape our images of Christmas with deep snow (crisp and even *etc*), cosy cottages, and poor people carrying bundles of fire wood, or lots of people skating on the frozen lake. This whole imagery was then merged into the Father Christmas idea and the importation of the Germanic Christmas tree via Queen Victoria's husband Prince Albert. Our deeper origins were more primeval and pagan, and fare less Christian. Early celebrations were linked to pagan mid-winter festivals, a reverence for winter-green plants such as Holly and Mistletoe: symbolising fertility and magic in the deep, dark, winter months. With death by cold or through starvation always just around the corner for many people this must have focused attention on questions like *'What's it all about*?' and *'Why am I here*?', and I'm sure *'Why is it so ****** cold*?' Ahhhh, this is what we mean by the joys of Christmas past, with Tiny Tim, roast chestnuts and a huge Turkey by a great log fire.

Winter Robin © Ian Rotherham

So back to the Robin on your Christmas card, and hopefully on your bird table (though in times past perhaps alongside the Turkey on the Christmas able as most small birds were considered fair game too).

Questions I have been asked

Which Mosquitoes bite and why? Most species don't bite and of those which do, it is the females. They need the blood as a source of protein for their eggs to develop. Believe it or not, most Mosquitoes get their food from vegetable matter such as rotting fruit.

Father Christmas and Christmas pudding

Our Christmas Robins now come in all shapes and sizes from cartoons images to stunning digital photographs. They symbolise Christmas and mid-winter with their cheerful disposition and bright red breast. Of course our Robins are famously more approachable than say French Robins and we at least like to think that this reflects the practice until recently of some French people in rural areas being likely to grab the Robin for the '*pot*'. Our birds reflect our friendly attitude to them and are safe in the knowledge that we are more likely to feed them than to feed on them. I wonder how true this is or is it Anglo-Saxon Francophobic rumour? As far as I know, none of my French friends has ever eaten a Robin. I think the Robin symbolises the optimistic and battling approach to life that our ancestors needed to get through the long dark winters. Remember no electric lights and no pollution from street lights; so these were long and dark winters. Our cheerful Robin was an emotive link to the brighter times of spring and summer, to perseverance; also as a bird of woodland and forest it may have been linked to primeval green spirits rooted deep in our psyche. Maybe this is a link to Father Christmas who before the Coca Cola PR team got their hands on him, was largely a green Father Christmas, perhaps even the *Green Man*, the spirit of the woods. As you sit down to Christmas dinner do think what it all means, why are we here? Spare a thought for the Robin and other wildlife that make it so special all year round.

Wild about New Year

It may not feel like it, but the nights are getting shorter and spring is on its way. This begins to have an impact on the wildlife across the region. The cold snap before Christmas pushed the birds into gardens and onto garden feeders. I'm sure that across the region you will have noticed good numbers of Blue Tits, Great Tits and the rest. The influx seems to have continued through the milder Christmas period. Birds visiting gardens provide a great opportunity for everyone to get involved in wildlife observation at the '*coal face*' as it were. This can even be the case if you can't get out and about, and perhaps one of the most important benefits we get from wildlife in the garden – nature contact and nature therapy. This is hugely important to many people but often something we just take for granted. On this vein, I've had a message from Joe Handley of Handsworth in Sheffield. Joe has noticed that his resident group of Sparrows have been eating peanuts rather than the seeds in the feeder next to the peanut one. However, earlier in the year (summer/autumn) they were feasting on seeds and leaving the peanuts alone! He wondered if anyone else had

noticed this. Could it be due to the higher energy content in the peanuts than in the seeds, and that they need this in the cold weather? For small birds in particular this is very important. In cold weather they lose a big part of their body weight each day just keeping warm. So let me know if your garden birds have been choosy about what they eat.

There's lots of wildlife around elsewhere too. Up on the moors it is worth watching for spectacular birds and in winter that means birds of prey. In recent years, our breeding Buzzard population has soared, literally. There's also a good chance of Peregrine; although it seems that persecution is still a problem, and unfortunately this is especially so in our region. You might also strike lucky with a Hen Harrier. These wonderful birds of prey took a tumble in the Peak District in the 1990s, but have recently begun to breed again. They are however, very vulnerable to illegal persecution at the nesting sites. Watch out for the brown females and youngsters, with just a white splash on the rump, and the steely grey males. In winter, there are communal roosts on favourite areas of moorland. Birds will come in at anything from an hour to two hours before dusk. A bit like the garden birds selecting their food for high energy, it is likely that these favoured roost sites are chosen because they are particularly sheltered. They also need to provide the best roosting habitat, such as dense leggy heather or dense rushes. Sometimes at sites such as this you can see a number of Harriers, and I recall in the 1980s, anything from three to ten birds plus a few Merlins thrown in. That would be most unlikely today. The Hen Harrier is one of our bird of prey species that unfortunately has bucked the trend of increasing; and since the 1980s numbers nationally have dropped. On the other hand, once we get into spring, if you head east you may see Marsh Harriers. These are the big brother of the smaller Hen Harrier, and used to be one of Britain's rarest birds. But (you guessed it!) they have increased dramatically and now number a few hundred breeding pairs. They do well in reedbeds and similar wetlands, so head east to the RSPB Nature Reserve at Blacktoft Sands in North Lincolnshire, one of Britain's best sites. If you decide to visit at this time of year then wrap up it can be very cold! If you fancy a birding trip more locally, then RSPB

Dearne Valley and the Old Moor Wetlands Centre is great and at this time of year can be spectacular. But try Rother Valley Country Park or Worsbrough too. They all have a lot to offer and have good access. Most of them, and especially Old Moor, boast good cafés; an essential when there's a cold northerly wind.

Try Gannets Café at RSPB Dearne Valley. © Ian Rotherham

Spring is on its way!

Ken Coldwell of Springfield Avenue says Ring Ouzels have arrived at Stanage Edge, after their long haul from southerly climes. This 'upland Blackbird' is typical of the moorland fringe and the gritstone edges, but now sadly quite rare; finding it hard to cope with nest-site disturbance. It is immortalised in local place-names like Ouzelden Clough in the Upper Derwent Valley. Ken and his wife saw three Ring Ouzels and it sounds like they were displaying, so fingers crossed! They may stay to breed or they might be migrants still heading further north. Although Ken saw his first Ouzels around fifty years ago, this was a first for his wife – and they were both very excited. For those not so familiar with bird watching this is a big deal when you see a new species for the first time. Also, it is fair to say that the Ring Ouzel is

a lovely bird – imagine a Blackbird but with a brilliant white collar. If you happen on a pair and they appear to be excited and displaying, then it is best not to hang around too long. They may be getting agitated because you are too close to their nest. Some bad news though in that their garden pond is low on mating Frogs this year; but I think this is localised as my pond is heaving.

I also had a letter from S. Stone of Chaucer Road in Sheffield. He has a large garden and feeds both the birds and local mammals; with a combination of nuts and table scraps it sounds like a Mecca for birds and apparently for Squirrels and Foxes. Anything left out overnight is hoovered up by the following morning. But Mr Stone also appreciates the wider countryside of Sheffield and the surrounding areas. Apparently as a young hiker he got around a bit and made the most (as many did and indeed still do) of the '*Golden Frame*'. I think that sometimes we take all this for granted, so it is good to be reminded of exactly how special it all is. Now at the age of 84 he looks back fondly of those times out in the countryside but still does his bit for nature in his back yard. His mother-in–law told him how when she was young she really enjoyed the scenery around the old River Don '*before they built all the works*'. Now that must've been a few years ago. I gather that Mr Stone's Uncle Sam was a lamplighter down Attercliffe after the 1914-1918 War. That's one of those jobs that you've heard about but have little idea of what is involved. I suppose there are a lot of similar skills and occupations that have slipped quietly away except in a few memories. I'd like to hear more.

I'm getting quite a lot of records of deer from the eastern part of Sheffield, and particularly of Roe Deer and the exotic little Muntjac; so please keep a look out and let me know what you see. The other obvious things at the moment are spring migrant birds arriving back and resident birds establishing territories; basically singing away like mad in the early hours of the morning. There are Magpies trampling on rooftops and gutters and throwing lumps of moss everywhere, and Sparrows and other smaller birds collecting soft materials for lining their nests. Mine love to collect the white, fluffy seed heads of the Pampas Grass. The Blackbirds are busy nest building and I suspect some will have young pretty soon. I've also had my first Sand Martins and Swallows back at places like Clumber Park in North Nottinghamshire. At Norton I've got my Canada Geese back on the local ponds and flying low over houses in earlier morning or late evening; a bit like a squadron of Lancaster Bombers. Combined with a Heron or two (today mobbed by an irate Carrion Crow) and looking and sounding a bit like a prehistoric Pterodactyl, it is all very exciting.

A final thought on Ouzels from Rev. Gilbert White in the 1700s - though rare, they were '*juicy and well flavoured*'.

Clumber Park Never Fails to Please

The National Trust is one of our key conservation bodies, both regionally and nationally, with over a million members and even more visitors to NT sites. One of my favourites is Clumber Park in north Nottinghamshire, the former house and landscape of the Dukes of Newcastle. This is parkland imposed onto the ancient woods and heaths of the greater Sherwood Forest, but then its house was largely demolished in the early twentieth century. The National Trust acquired the site in the 1940s, and actually paid for some of the purchase price by selling some of the

great Oaks for timber. How times change. Nobody would dream of doing that now. However, since then they have done a great job of gradually restoring the old stables and the garden areas. With a café and shop, and a garden centre, the Trust offers a range of pleasant diversions for a day out. These not only attract visitors but importantly help fund the vital conservation work. Again this site would be a challenge to visit by public transport, so most people visit by car, and if you are not a member then there is an entry charge. (The answer, if you can afford it, is to join the National Trust and get free entry every time).

Gadwall Duck at Clumber. © Ian Rotherham

So, if you've never been to Clumber Park, what does it offer? I think one of the big attractions is the variety of wide open space but in a more intimate setting than say the Peak District. Although this is a much modified landscape you can imagine these woodlands and heaths as a setting for Robin Hood; a romantic and historic place. There are numerous walks that are clearly signposted and suit all ages and levels of mobility, and they are through a rich and exciting environment. The favourite walk, though it is not compulsory, is around the lake itself. This will take an hour or so at a comfortable walking pace. There are other routes that branch off and intertwine throughout this large site. You can also cycle with your own bike or hire one from the Trust.

There are then three main wildlife habitats in the Park – acid heath and grassland, woodland, and the lake and river. The woods include ancient Oak woods, planted areas with Beech and Sweet Chestnut plus loads of other exotic species, and conifer plantations. Along the lakeside and riverside are rich areas of wet Alder wood – nowadays a rarity and I've found

Harvest Mouse here. Each area has its own distinctive 'feel' and its own wildlife. The lake is a magnet for water-birds from flocks of screaming Black-headed Gulls, to stately Mute Swans, and gaggles of noisy Canada Geese, to ducks such as Mallard, Teal, Pochard, and even Gadwall. There are good numbers of both Great Crested Grebe and Little Grebe. With very little effort at Clumber you can notch up a good list of birds seen – if you're into that sort of thing. The woodland and heath areas are rich in typical woodland or woodland edge birds – Great Tits, Blue Tits, Coal Tits, and the rare Marsh Tit. Along the river banks watch out for Long-tailed Tits and both Siskin and Redpoll. You also have a good chance of Great Spotted and Green Woodpeckers, and of course the now ubiquitous Nuthatch. Open areas have Skylark and even (though rarely) Woodlark, along with Yellowhammers and Common Whitethroats. The latter is a warbler and a summer visitor to us. In the wooded habitats their cousins the Willow Warblers and Chiffchaff, and the Blackcap and Garden Warbler will be in full song. In the 1970s, Clumber was still a stronghold for Nightingale in the dense areas of planted *Rhododendron*. Alas no more, they have long since gone after the *Rhododendron scrub* was well and truly '*bashed*'.

Ruddy Duck. © Ian Rotherham

Back to the waterside and you may, if you are very lucky, catch a glimpse of the now rare Ruddy Duck. Don't tell anyone though. Like the *Rhododendron* they are an alien species and so are not approved of. They are on borrowed time, so get to see them whilst you can!

Cuckoos and Campion

Cuckoo from a Victorian print

High over Norton swooped two Cuckoos, with their long tails and scythe-like wings sharply pointed and angled back. I couldn't hear them, but shape and flight were distinctive. With heathland decline and the expansion of cities into countryside, Cuckoos have decreased over recent decades. But here, close to the beautiful Moss Valley and not too far from the Peak District moors, there's still a chance see or at least hear them at this time of year. Around Charnock I used to hear them most years in late spring or early summer. And it is certainly that time of year with roadsides and woodland edges resplendent in wild flowers. Two are especially obvious at the moment, the Cow Parsley and the Red Campion. The former a member of the Carrot family with tall upright stems and large but delicate 'umbels' of tiny white flowers, has many common names including Queen Anne's Lace, Lady's Lace, Fairy Lace, Mother Die, Kek, Kecksie, Hedge Parsley, and even Rabbit Meat.

Fancy that

What's in a name?

The Black-headed Gull or *Larus ridibundus* doesn't really exist. It has a brown head for about half the year, and a white blotchy one for the rest. Confused?

Red Campion. © Ian Rotherham

According to Richard Mabey the name Queen Anne's Lace was because when she travelled the country one May, apparently people said the roads had been decorated for her. Suffering from asthma the Queen would travel the countryside around Kensington (then still fields and hedges) in search of clean air. She and her ladies carried lace pillows and so there is an alternative explanation. Cow Parsley basically means the Parsley that's not as good as real Parsley! Anyway I would agree with Richard Mabey that this is perhaps the most important flower in the English landscape – at least in May and June, livening up almost every patch of neglected ground and every roadside, hedgerow or verge; and exceptionally pretty. There may be confusion sometimes with the very poisonous Hemlock, a member of the same family but with evil-looking purple blotches on the stem and a very unpleasant smell. Not good unless like the Ancient Greeks you want to get rid of someone!

It is complemented by another wayside flower, and one of my favourites, the Red Campion. It too has other names like Adder's Flower (as this and its cousin Ragged Robin were used to cure snake venom), Robin Hood, or Cuckoo Flower. I presume the last name ties in with my original observation of this being the time of year for the Cuckoo and the Campion. When abundant, along a woodland edge perhaps or on a sea cliff like Flamborough, Red Campion is a stunning sight. It hybridises with its close relative the White Campion to produce a range from pure white to bright pinkish red. White Campion is much more a plant of disturbed ground and the hybrids often occur in intermediate areas. There's a whole swathe of hybrid Campion on the roadside near Worksop where the by-pass cuts through towards Clumber Park. There you'll see a variety of soft pinks and white all mixed in together. Go into one of our local ancient woodlands though and all you get is the pure Red Campion. That is the woodland plant and the hybrids are filtered out by nature and ecology very effectively; each plant to its own little niche. Apparently this was also called Mother Dee or Mother Die with the suggestion that if you picked it would bring misfortune upon your parents. Apparently in the Isle of Man it was a flower of the fairies was therefore unlucky and should not be picked. In parts of Wales it was called the Snake Flower and people were convinced that they would be attacked by a snake if they brought it into the house. I wonder if this somehow links to the idea of it as a cure for snake bite. Another concern was that if you picked Red Campion flowers there would be a storm of thunder and lightning and so it was called Thunder Flower. Have you any memories or recollections of local names or folklore concerned with either Cow Parsley or Red Campion? Perhaps like the good folk of Sussex you used its '*corrosive juice*' to cure your warts, or in Gloucestershire to get rid of corns. Anyway, let me know.

Wild about Longshaw

One of my favourite walking areas is the Longshaw estate and the Burbage Valley that lies adjacent. In fact this was almost my first place to go walking on the moors after the Rivelin Valley. Now managed by the National Trust and by Sheffield City Council, these moors and woods are a wonderful recreational and conservation area. As a very small child I have a vivid recollection of a tethered goat grazing in the plantation south of Longshaw Lodge, not far from the Grouse Inn. I wonder if anyone else remembers that. I was very impressed, but then I was very small and after all you didn't see a '*wild*' goat every day of the week in Meersbrook! I also have memories of the first impression of the crags and tors of upper Burbage Valley and it seemed to me to be like a great medieval castle. We spent most of the day leaping from boulder to boulder; I suspect risking life and limb but getting nothing worse than a few cuts and bruises.

I was out there recently and had a real treat; a pair of Stonechats. This is the cousin of the Whinchat I mentioned the other week, but is rather rarer. The male is a particularly stunning bird with a very upright stance typical of the chats, and strong black head with orange red and bright white stripes. They tend to perch atop branches or other vegetation flicking their tail and making the '*tak tak tak*' call. The Stonechat is never common with us and is a bird much more frequently seen further south. The Gorse-topped cliffs of Cornwall or West Wales are its favourite haunts, and you can see several pairs at once. But they are less common as easterly as this, and numbers also vary a lot from year to year. Maybe they are benefiting from the warmer winters and longer summers we are experiencing. Good to see though and I hope they stop to breed.

Then, battling up the valley against a searing cold wind, the view was splendid, with the gritstone crags etched in snow. Then up out of nowhere appeared a Little Owl; also known to older country folk as the '*Frenchie*', '*Frenchman*', or '*French Owl*'. It was as you might expect introduced to Britain from France in the early 1900s, and was considered by gamekeepers as vermin and an alien to be exterminated ruthlessly. However, a detailed study showed that it did no harm to game and probably benefiting farmers by eating various pest species. Since then it has been tolerated, and for most birdwatchers as sighting is a bit special. They are a little gem of a bird. Not much bigger than a Blackbird but with big yellow eyes and a typical predator's behaviour, even if it is only pocket–sized. The Owl treated us to a decent view at close quarters and then was off with a gentling undulating flight, to appear again some distance away on a big

boulder. Close too, it bobs up and down as if nervously assessing the situation; friend or foe? Deciding that discretion was the order of the day, it was away and we didn't see it again.

The so-called '*Magic Mushroom*' a Longshaw special. © Ian Rotherham

The Raven

A bird at home on bleak moorland is the Raven, for many decades extinct in the Peak District as a breeding bird. For many years the only sightings were of occasional winter visitors. But they are back and a good thing too. The Raven really is a magnificent bird and the moors would be the less without them. They have done pretty well in recent years ands can now be seen or heard on most of the edges. In fact you generally hear them before you see them. The deep, guttural '*pruk pruk, pronk pronk*' carries for half a mile or more on a quiet day with the right wind. The big daddy of the Crow world, the Raven is a bird of mythology and of symbolism, and is very deeply engrained in our culture. People talk of the benefits of '*being close to nature*', and having two Ravens overhead at Burbage I think hits the spot.

Wild Longshaw. © Ian Rotherham

Take a stroll at Carsington Water

Situated just outside the Peak District National Park, Carsington Water Reservoir was hugely controversial during its planning. Like many reservoirs, most local people really didn't want it. Furthermore, when the original construction was found to be unstable as it was situated on a geological fault, I recall local environmentalists being quietly amused. However, much has changed and this huge water-body that submerged an entire Derbyshire valley in the early 1990s is now a highly valued wildlife,

countryside recreational and tourism site. Since it first opened it has exceeded expectations with over a million visitors each year. If you haven't been, then I suggest that you do; although getting there by bus will test you, so it is probably a car journey, and around 45-60 minutes from Sheffield. What you find there is a great day out for everyone from individuals to families or groups. There is plenty of parking, and pretty good restaurants and cafés, and a few outdoor clothing, gift shops and bookshops. The only visitor charge is for the car park. Once there, then there are well-made and effectively signposted walks around the Reservoir; anything from a couple of miles to eight miles or so. There are bird-watching hides and usually a few rangers and local volunteers around to guide you if lost, or to help identify the abundant birdlife. This is a good spot for commoner countryside birds like finches and titmice, but also for more rare species like Tree Sparrow – here in abundance. Watch out in the fields and hedgerows for Yellowhammer, Bullfinches, Long-tailed Tits, and Linnets. The landscape here mixes ancient hedgerows and lanes, and old meadows, in some cases with medieval 'ridge and furrow', and newly-created plantations of Willow, Alder and other scrub. Good sized old Oak trees sit next to young planted Birch. Check these older trees for Treecreepers hunting tiny insects in the deep-furrowed bark. Listen too for both Great Spotted Woodpecker and Green Woodpecker, the latter with its typical yaffling laughing call. Wait for the territorial drumming on old dead branches.

But Carsington's claim to fame is perhaps more for its water-birds. This is a big area of water and in the landscape at a distance appears more like a Cumbrian lake. With the water comes a range of wild birds, a changing kaleidoscope with the seasons. In spring you will see the commoner duck species, and many of them breeding here. Mallard and Tufted Duck are abundant, but there are others such as Teal and of course Moorhens and the ever-aggressive Coot. The latter is a bird with a serious attitude problem. There are lots of geese, but mostly Canada Geese and feral Grey Lags; nice all the same. You also have a good chance of Grey Heron and even Kingfisher. In the shallower bays along the edge of the lake, listen and watch for Little Grebe. A nice thing about Carsington is the juxtaposition of the lake and adjacent meadows, and the wading birds just love this. They can loaf in the fields and then flight over to the water's edge, calling loudly as they do so. The high-pitched repeated call of Redshank mingle pleasantly with the bubbling Curlew, whilst Lapwing (or Green Plover) call, a plaintive '*peewit*', and tumble with their spectacular display over their breeding meadows. It is the sort of stuff that makes you feel good to be alive. (Watch out too for the huge flocks of Lapwings which gather in pour lowland areas in winter; sometimes numbering several thousand and with a distinctive flickering flight of what look like black and white wings). For the smaller birds though, as the local Sparrowhawk and Kestrel patrol the hedgerows and the reservoir edge, they need to keep their heads down if they wish to stay that way.

The Lapwing by Charles Tunnicliffe

   In sheltered areas of damp woodland, with sunlight flecks dappling the vegetation, the earlier butterflies look for nectar sources and to establish breeding territories. Green-veined White and Orange-tip Butterflies love spring

flowers like Honesty, Hedge Garlic, and Lady's Smock; favourite breeding plants on which to lay their eggs. (Planting these in your garden may be enough to tempt these beautiful little butterflies in. At least it is worth a try). The first Bluebells are also showing and attracting the attentions of large female Bumblebees. Spring is here.

A Walk in the Rain

Where to go on a rainy day? Well a good walk that is firm under foot is along the Peak Park's Monsal Trail. Mostly along disused railway lines, this route cuts through wonderful Derbyshire countryside, and of course it is free. Go to either the old Bakewell Railway Station, or to the car park at Hassop Station Bookshop. From there you are on to an easy walk that can either take you further afield or be a simple 3-4 mile stroll. The great thing is that it suited to all users from old to young, and from walkers to horse riders and cyclists. There's lots of information on the web; such as: www. thepeakdistrict.info/cycling.php with plenty of stuff about where to go and how to hire a bike *etc*. Whilst on a nice day and especially at a weekend it can be busy, if you choose your time carefully, it is pretty quiet. Following the line of the former Midland Railway from Blackwell Mill Cottages to around one kilometre past the old Bakewell Railway Station, it is around sixteen miles or twenty kilometres. The trail mostly follows the path of the River Wye, and so offers spectacular scenic views. The eastern end of the trail is accessible to cyclists but the western section; with parts around Chee Tor quite difficult even for walkers. Between Litton Mill and Cressbrook Mill the Trail follows a concessionary footpath along which cycling is forbidden. The route has a quite turbulent history. When the Victorian railway through the valley was proposed, pioneering conservationists led by John Ruskin were distraught and opposed it; much as they did the railways to the Lake District. Today though, it is accepted as a core part of the landscape. Indeed, recent proposals (now abandoned) which were to reopen the line as a tourist railway route, generated concerns from conservationists.

Monsal Trail near Bakewell. © Ian Rotherham

Anyway, back to Hassop Station, with its bookshop and café, the ideal bolt-hole on a wet day in winter. But venture out of the shelter of the railway embankments, the panoramic views and the well made path mean for a pleasant walk whatever the weather. You can also get a feel for the changing seasons if you come here on a regular basis. The embankments have loads of wild flowers from hedgerow and woodland species to grassland and marsh. And along with these, at the right time of year, you can expect insects such as butterflies in abundance. There are lots of Rabbit burrows, and that means Foxes too. Walking along you'll pick up the strong musk smell of the adult Fox. You can see their runs, and those of Badgers, trodden out through the rank vegetation and leading off into secret groves or a more distinct spinney.

At this time of year there are flocks of small birds in abundance. I had around fifty to sixty Goldfinches chattering and buzzing excitedly in the treetops. They were probably exchanging information on good places to feed, or perhaps favoured roosting sites for the late afternoon. They interacted briefly with a small flock of Long-tailed Tits, in body size our smallest bird at about 2½ inches. Their soft churr or trill is quite distinctive. In a big Sycamore Tree just off the Trail, there was a flock of thrush-like birds. On closer inspection this was around thirty Starlings, again very noisy, and a smaller and separate group of three Redwings. The latter are similar to our resident song Thrush, perhaps a little smaller, and with a white stripe above the eye, and a red flank. With their larger cousin the Fieldfare, the Redwing is a winter visitor down

from the north. They love berry bushes such as Hawthorn, and Wild Roses with their ripe rose hips that line the embankments in abundance.

With all this activity you might expect predators around too. Well they do have to eat; sorry to all the lovers of small birds!! You'll not be disappointed as there's a good chance of Common Buzzard, Kestrel, or Sparrowhawk. Late afternoon or early evening, if all is quiet watch out for the local Fox too.

Kingfishers and Wild Daffodils

One of my favourite walks is along the Cromford Canal from Cromford Mill, just south of Matlock Bath. I was out there a couple of weeks ago, and along with numerous pairs of Little Grebe or Dabchick, hidden away on the fair bank of the canal, well away from the old Mill, were Wild Daffodils. These are quite a rarity for us, and amazingly there were already bursting into flower. Now that is early! This is a lovely and easy gentle stroll, with wild flowers, including another local rarity Mistletoe, and the Lesser Teasel. There's a good chance of waterside birds such as Kingfisher, and the ubiquitous Moorhens and Coots. I also had good views of a splendid male Grey Wagtail, with its bright yellow, white and black markings, and of course its slate-grey back. But here I think is the best site to get close to see Little Grebes. If you stand still by the water's edge they will give a complete performance with underwater swimming, and excited displays between the male and female. They are holding territories and each stretch of a hundred metres or so of canal has its own resident pair. They make a very distinctive high-pitched sort of whistling call, and if you learn to recognise this then you will hear them before you see them.

On the subject of Kingfishers, I had an email from the appropriately named Edward (Ted) Wren, and yes he does have Wrens in his garden too! He was recounting his sightings of Kingfishers; '*I was working at Neepsend in the early 1980's, and I used to go for lunchtime walks from Hillfoot Bridge along Club Mill Road. Several times I saw a Kingfisher flash across the Don. On one occasion I looked over a wall at the bank side to see a Kingfisher about six feet below. It made two dives (unsuccessful)* into the river before it saw me, and off it went. My last sighting was earlier this year. It was perched over the mill race near the fire station at Bakewell, ignoring the people watching it from about five yards away. I live on the Dronfield side of the Sheffield/Derbyshire green belt and I occasionally see a heron flying over the back gardens around breakfast time. It has perched on a tree in my garden, and on my neighbour's garage.' It really is wonderful to be able to see such splendid birds so close. A message from Neil O'Loughlin, from the east of our region was along the same lines. '*I am not a bird watcher as such, but I know a Kingfisher when I see one. Two weekends ago my wife and I were just walking over the A638 road bridge over the River Torne at Rossington Bridge, about 4 miles south of Doncaster, when we spotted a Kingfisher which had just flown under the bridge from the southwest and emerged to fly north east along the river for about 40 to 50 yards before we lost sight of it.*' Yes, they are pretty much unmistakeable, and it is good that they are doing so well. It is good too to hear from readers over to the east. There are some fantastic wildlife sites across that way and I'd like to hear more about them.

and with warmer summers they are doing well. We are getting more Hornet records, and so they might turn up. Hornets favour dead trees and rot pockets for their nests, and they are a seriously big Wasp; more about them later.

Useful tips: *How to avoid being bitten by Midges*

- ❖ Keep on the move and if you can find an area with a breeze that helps enormously.
- ❖ Generally try wearing white or lighter coloured clothes.
- ❖ Keep in the sun if possible.
- ❖ Apparently you should eat loads of **MARMITE** each day for two weeks before your trip.
- ❖ Keep away from the worst areas from June to August – the Scottish Highlands of course, but I recall Blackamoor being particularly bad too.
- ❖ Avoid late evening and early morning.

Hornet '*the real deal*'.© **Ian Rotherham**

Jenny Buchan-Smith contacted me because she was concerned about seeing a '*Hornet*' buzzing around her bathroom. She wondered if this was to do with climate change, but she was rather taken aback by what entomologists would describe as a '*large vespid*' (sounds like a type of motor scooter). Well without going to investigate I think we can be sure that it was not a Hornet – though I would be excited if it was. This was a queen Wasp just woken up after hibernating in the attic or perhaps in the airing cupboard. There've been loads of them about

Autumn colours at Froggatt. © Ian Rotherham

SHEFFIELD AND THE PEAK THROUGH THE SEASONS

Celebrate the Seasons

I suspect that for many people one of the rather wonderful, but often almost unrecognised aspects of nature is its seasonal variation. It is so fundamental to us that we perhaps take it for granted. So for example, we have a rich array and diversity of wildlife and flowers that light up and characterise each period of time over the year. Sometimes the weather alters the emphasis and we have especially striking periods of maybe a particular flower or even an abundance of a specific insect, such as for example swarms of Ladybirds and infestations of Aphids. But even so there are certain trends and particular times that make up the season. Probably somewhere deep in the human psyche we need the variation and the predictability, and even the unusual as a diversion from the norm. The

British are famous for talking about the weather, which we have a lot of; and this is the same general idea. And within this broad pattern of our relationship with the seasons there are particular plants and animals which we await, that we look forward to, and for which we note their timely arrival or emergence. The great thing about this seasonal kaleidoscope is that it occurs in every garden, on every patch of 'waste' land, and especially along every roadside. So I suggest that we savour each moment and every predictable yet unique event. Even the commonplace becomes special when it is on your 'patch'. Contact with nature and an awareness of the seasons is something that we have been in danger of losing in the hustle and bustle of modern living. I think too, that to appreciate say the summer, your need a good cold winter; to anticipate spring then you have to have the autumn. It is nature's great cycle.

A spring walk on Sheffield's Wild Side

Despite the cold snap of recent weeks, spring is most definitely in the air, and it is early again. We've had Snowdrops and Primroses out in January, and I had Wild Daffodils in flower in mid-February. That really is very early. There's been a spate of sightings of Queen Wasps; awaking from hibernation and frightening people who think they have a Hornet in the house. There've also been records of butterflies such as Red Admiral and Tortoiseshell emerging from hibernation, often in closet or in the attic. They re-appear with the first warm days of early spring.

Now with gardens full of Crocuses and dwarf Daffodils, the local woods, gardens, and parks are full of birds singing as they set up and defend their breeding territories. The noisiest at present are probably the Great Tits, but Blue Tits are pretty active too, along with Chaffinches and Greenfinches. The Robin, Wren and Dunnock tend to sing right the way through the winter anyway and in the evening Blackbirds going to roost are especially vociferous. In the evening now you will hear Tawny Owls; and if you stand quietly in your back garden you may have a good chance of seeing them too. They are one of the earliest of our breeding birds, and highly aggressive around the nest. The pioneering bird photographer Eric Hosking famously lost an eye to at Tawny Owl attack. The other evening and night time serenades are from local Foxes that are actively defending territories at this time of year. They can produce a whole range of calls, and screams and howls that can be quite disturbing until you know what it is.

Watch out is the garden too for Goldfinches that will love to come to Teasel heads or to special feeders with Niger Seed. They have increased dramatically in recent years and are one of the success stories of the bird world. I've noticed recently that Bullfinches have taken to joining the Goldfinches on the feeder. These really are one of our special birds but unfortunately are not common and have gone down in numbers. This may be as we have lost most of our old orchards and many older fruit trees. If you do have an orchard near you, or perhaps old fruit trees in the garden, then look out for one of our newest arrivals: the Ring-Necked Parakeet. They have joined us all the way from the tropics, but via pet shops in London where they were deliberately released to the wild. They are doing very well; seen in our areas around Chesterfield, Beighton, Gleadless, and Meersbrook.

It's that May Blossom Time

It seems to happen very quickly. Suddenly all the hedgerows and woodland edges, all the areas of fields and scrub, and even up on the moorland fringe, is heaving with May Blossom, the Hawthorn. 'Quick-thorn', or White Thorn, has taken over the world with its wonderful massed flower-heads and its overpowering fragrance; a heady experience, and this natural wonder is free for all to enjoy. We have two main species of thorns wild in Britain, the Hawthorn (out now) and the Blackthorn that was in flower some weeks ago. There is another Hawthorn called the Midland Hawthorn, a rather special rare shrub of ancient woods and woodland edge, but that's a story for another time. I think the Hawthorn is one of those special plants that we just take for granted. They generally grow to only a modest or even small size, but some of the Hawthorns out on the moors west of Sheffield and Barnsley are probably much older than they look. I suspect that some are several hundred years old. Many were planted in the imposed hedgerows of the 'Enclosures' in the 1700s and 1800s, to form the typical patchwork hedges of middle England. There is a big chunk of social history in that landscape. This was how the commons were wrested from the commoners and enclosed into smaller fields for private landowners. They may be rather pretty today but they were often bitterly resented in the 1700s.

Useful tips

A Laurel wreath placed on your house door will prevent disease from entering the household.

Keeping a Bay Leaf in your mouth all day will avert bad luck. It will also deflect many otherwise pointless conversations.

May Blossom. © Ian Rotherham

To best appreciate Hawthorns get out to an open setting such as a scrubby heathland or perhaps a grassy dale side in Derbyshire. Here on a sunny day when in full bloom they are a splendid sight; you'll hear myriad buzzing insects feasting on pollen and nectar. Listen again and you'll probably hear a Chaffinch singing from a high branch, hidden from view by swollen bunches of brilliant white flowers and pale green leaves. In Hawthorn scrub there's a chance of the warblers especially Garden Warbler or Common Whitethroat or even Lesser Whitethroat. Chiffchaff and Willow Warbler are also now in full song. By the autumn of course these same Hawthorns will be important feeding stations for migrant birds re-fuelling for the long haul south, and then for the winter Thrushes feasting before they head back north. In spring when the leaves first burst through children used to eat them as '*bread and cheese*', and they were a useful source of Vitamin C for poor children after a long winter. This of course was when we had to make our own entertainment and before TV and computer games.

However, I think that to appreciate the heady, almost sickly fragrance of the Hawthorn it is best to experience it down an old winding lane with ancient hedges and overhanging branches suffused with abundant flowers and overpowering aroma. That said, not everyone likes it. Apparently for some it smells of rotting meat, or the stench associated with the plague. It doesn't smell like that to me but perhaps I'm one of the lucky ones. It was also considered unlucky in some areas, and bringing cut Hawthorn flowers into a household could cause a death in the family. This brings a whole new meaning to '*say it with flowers*'! (A bit like the graffiti '*Say it with flowers – send her a Trifid*'). On the other hand Hawthorn was supposed to protect you against witches; so not all bad then. The berries are still collected by herbalists to make medicines for circulatory disorders like angina and high blood pressure, and also varicose veins.

People get confused with the Thorns and with Blackthorn in particular. The bark of Blackthorn is distinctly dark and when the brilliant white flowers emerge the plant is not yet in leaf. The white of the flowers makes the bark stand out as jet black of the '*Black-Thorn*'. The other big difference is in the way the two shrubs grow. Hawthorn is generally a typical small tree, whereas Blackthorn tends to send out masses of suckers and form dense, impenetrable thickets. These are often great habitat for animals such as Fox and Badger, with the sharp spines protecting against intruders. Blackthorn also fruits as berries giving us the Sloe of Sloe Gin.

The roadsides are now full of the white flowers of Cow Parsley and the pink flowers of Red Campion. Bluebells, both Spanish and native are still around but are going over, to be replaced by the flowers of early summer. There are also White Butterflies skipping along the same hedges, the woodland edge and in gardens. Watch out for the Green-veined white butterfly with its delicate tracery of green on the underside of its hind wings, or the pretty Orange-tip Butterfly as it searches for its host plants of Honesty or Hedge Garlic.

Finally, 'watch out there's a deer about'. I'm getting very exciting records of both native Roe Deer and the alien Muntjac; especially around south and east Sheffield. Do let me know what you see around your patch.

Fancy that

The first Primroses and Cowslips in spring tell us that summer is on its way. These are some of our prettiest and most evocative flowers, but the Cowslip's name is less than romantic. It actually is derived from the Old English '*cuslyppe*', which means '*cow dung*'. In old meadows the Cowslips flourish in amongst the dung pats. The last native Primrose site in Sheffield was deliberately destroyed by site owners *Massey Truck Engineering* at Holbrook in the late 1990s. Well done guys.

Summer Birds and other Wildlife

There's lots of summer wildlife about the region and in recent weeks young birds have been leaving their nests and taking their first tentative flutters. In hedgerows, woods, parks and gardens you'll see flocks of young Blue Tits and Great Tits, and perhaps the occasional Coal tit or Nuthatch. The young are tatty versions of the adults with blotchy markings and feathers sticking out untidily; some look very odd, the bird equivalent of a '*bad hair day*'. Family groups merge into larger flocks and the different and excited noises and calls generate a real cacophony. My Great Spotted Woodpeckers are regulars on the garden peanut feeder. They are joined by a pair of brilliantly-coloured Bullfinches and delightful Goldfinches on the seed hopper. These little contacts with nature on the doorstep are so very special and I get lots of letters and emails from listeners about what they see in their gardens or close to home. There are reports of Starlings, Woodpigeons, Collared Doves, Magpies, Robins, Blue Tits and Great Tits, Greenfinches and Chaffinches, and larger birds like Jackdaws and Magpies, all in local gardens. Even Carrion Crows will come down to feed but are usually very wary. It seems that Jackdaws in particular are coming into our gardens more frequently. Like all the Crow family the Jackdaw is intelligent and inquisitive. It has a distinctive grey patch on the back of its head and amazingly steel blue eyes and will often come onto rooftops in urban areas, a replacement for their natural habitat of cliffs and crags, and in some places they are quite approachable. I've had listeners report them nesting regularly in a favoured chimney stack. Jays are also seen more commonly in gardens though back in the 1970s they were still quite rare. They seem to have increased dramatically and are also bolder. The Jays are especially interesting and Jan Peel at Loxley reported one feeding on a nut-holder. I also had one feeding on a peanut holder in my garden at Norton and it looked most odd hanging upside down on the feeder. This behaviour only lasted for about three months and I've never seen it again, even though the Jays visit quite frequently. I'd be interested to know if anyone else has observed this. Birds do experiment and sometimes adopt new feeding habits and some listeners will remember when the Blue Tits used to peck through the foil tops of milk bottles to get the cream. Of course that was when we had old-fashioned milk bottles and doorstep deliveries!

With the poor weather we've had it has not been a good year for butterflies, but there are some Dragonflies about. In Derbyshire the other weekend I saw a female Broad-bodied Chaser Dragonfly; pretty stunning nothing compared with male. Watch-out for the Kingfisher-blue male Broad-bodied Chaser, out and about near you and unmistakable.

If you are over towards the Peak District side of the region then roadsides are now profuse with wild flowers. The Marsh Orchids are now finishing but have been brilliant, and whole swathes of roadside verge are covered with the bright blue flowers of Meadow Cranesbill and the yellow of the delicate Lady's Bedstraw or its cousin Crosswort – look for the tiny yellow flowers in the shape of across and neatly arranged in whorls around the stem. Another striking pant to watch out for is one of the Cow Parsley Family (the Umbellifers) aptly called the '*Common Hogweed*'. Take a deep sniff at the massed head of white flowers and you'll find out why!!

Meadow Cranesbill. © Ian Rotherham

If you're up on the moors west of Sheffield and Barnsley then keep your eyes peeled and listen for the deep, guttural '*pruk pruk pronk pronk*', with a bit of luck a large black Crow will appear: the Raven. Once extinct locally but now making a welcome return, I saw six over one of the Peak District edges, presumably a family party. What a treat to see them so close to home!

Late summer: the time of heather and meadows

Roadsides, lanes and what we used to call '*waste land*' have been full of wild flowers and their attendant butterflies and day-flying moths. Striking swathes of Rosebay Willowherb now stand proud along roadsides and disused railway lines, and on our 'urban commons'. Also known as Fireweed or Railway Flower, this distinctive plant is the food stuff of the Elephant Hawk Moth, as big as your finger and with scary 'eyes' on the front of its body and a curious hooked tail at the other end. The former serve to frighten off would-be predators and the latter to fend of tiny wasps that parasitize the big fat caterpillars; one of nature's less pleasant stories. They eat their live host slowly and from the inside! Believe it or not the Rosebay was once very rare, a plant of extensive heaths and of upland moors. In the late 1800s, the Yorkshire Naturalist's Union organised a special field excursion to Thorne Moors near Doncaster just to see this rare plant. It spread rapidly though along the Victorian railway lines, helped by regular fires caused by steam engines, and then benefited greatly from '*disturbance*' during the blitz.

Rosebay in bloom. © Ian Rotherham

There is also a final twist to this story in that the Rosebay we see today is much larger and more aggressive (in the way it spreads, not that it will attack you!), than that found in the 1800s. It is believed that another variety of the same species, bigger and stronger from America, came into Britain with cargoes of cotton and other materials in ships. This met and hybridized with the puny native to give it what we call '*hybrid vigour*'. So there you have it, a few things to consider next time you look at a clump of Rosebay Willowherb.

In areas of undisturbed meadows on roadside and sympathetically-managed farmland there is a whole set of wild flowers that flower and seed in phases throughout the summer. Now is the time of the Harebell. Talking to Rony recently we wondered about the meaning of the plant name '*Harebell*'. They are out all along the roadsides in the Peak District and on old, unimproved grassland too. This is the Scottish '*Bluebell*' and related to garden Campanulas. Its scientific name is *Campanula* (meaning bell-shaped) *rotundifolia* (meaning round-leaved). The latter is a bit confusing because if you examine the leaves on the flower-stem they are actually rather thin and not round at all. You need to look for the basal leaves hidden in a little rosette at ground level, and yes, they are sort of round. Apparently in Scotland the Harebell, also known as '*The Old Man's Bell*' or '*The Devil's Bell*', was feared and generally left alone. Called '*The Witch Bell*', '*The Witch-thimble*', it was not to be picked. In Ireland too it was regarded as dangerous and was the thimble of the *puca* or goblin, *bròg na-cubhaig* in Gaelic. In south-west England it was '*The Fairy Bell*' and in the Isle of Man '*The Fairies Thimble*', associated with things magical. So the question is this. Is the name linked to the magical and superstitious nature of the Hare – also feared and revered in folklore and in superstition? The Hare was regarded as '*a witch animal*' and so is the name '*Harebell*' from this sort of connection? If you have any idea or have any memories or old names or even uses for the little *Campanula*, then do let us know.

Harebells. © Ian Rotherham

This is what it's all about!

Now is the time of the heather and the moors, though we haven't always viewed them as '*a good thing*' or even as beautiful. Daniel Defoe, travelling in 1725, described the moors above Chatsworth as '*...a waste and a howling wilderness*'. I recall talking to a senior manager at the then British Tissues plant at Oughtibridge back in the 1980s, about how they were tipping

Peak district moors. © Ian Rotherham

paper pulp waste across swathes of the Peak National Park, across Bradfield Parish and of course Sheffield. His response was that he didn't like moorland, it was too bleak and it would be better as improved grassland and planted trees. Perhaps Defoe was visiting on a bad day and the guy at British Tissues needed to acclimatise and appreciate our wonderful South Pennine landscape. (And yes for all those Bradfield Parish Councillors who apparently think I'm a Luddite, it is fantastic and it is beautiful and we must **all** do our bit responsibly to conserve it for future generations. We'll come back to this later). I sometimes take groups of first year students to Stanage Edge for their first Peak District visit and ask them to describe what they see and how they feel. Interestingly, about 50-80% of them think that it is fantastic and this is a big reason why they've come to Sheffield Hallam University to study. Generally around 20-50% of the students, mostly from lowland England or from warmer climes, think it is a god-forsaken spot and they never wish to visit again! This is something to ponder on in terms of perceptions and values.

Moors, heaths and blanket bogs can be bleak, especially in winter, but even then they retain a latent and brooding magnificence. In late July through to September they burst out into the most wonderful landscape of purple heather. The fragrance is heavy in the air, especially if you get a still, warm, humid day; the smell of heather honey and old English mead. For just a few weeks the landscape is transformed beyond imagination into a stunning suffusion of purples, reds, mauves, and pinks. Following from the more localised flowering of Common Cotton-grass which turns the blanket bogs snow-white in June and July, this is surely one of Nature's miracles that we should all be proud of and indeed grateful for. My research on landscape history at Sheffield Hallam University shows how the moors and heaths used to extend right across the region and down into the lowlands; imagine that. From the late 1700s onwards, whole areas were swept away by agricultural '*improvement*', and the unique heritage was largely banished to the uplands. In late medieval times, Barnsley for example, was known as '*Black Barnsley*' not because of smoke pollution or even because of coal mining, but because the landscape setting was dark with heather moorland. You can still find occasional moorland and heath sites down in the lower-lying areas. Try Wickfield Heath in Sheffield's *Shire Brook Valley Nature Reserve* for our best local site, or even Houghton Common high above Grimethorpe, east of Barnsley. Further east there are of course the expanses of Thorne and Hatfield Moors, or at least what remains after the efforts of the horticultural peat extractors and mineral companies have taken their fill.

Heather. © Ian Rotherham

To appreciate and enjoy this most vivid and pleasant of Nature's free spectacles then most of us must go west to the Pennines and Peak District, and August is the time. Stand atop one of the Gritstone edges and drink deep of the view and of the overpowering fragrance. Heather stands out against dark rocks and even darker peat; the '*big sky*' reflecting and infusing the landscape with further colour; the breeze lifting the gorgeous scent of heaths and other blossoms, sometimes carrying it several miles to lower-lying land to the east; a reminder perhaps of what once was. But surely if we need a reason to conserve our wildlife heritage, to take responsibility for our rich and unique environment, then this must be it. The pioneers who gave us access to the moors and fought to establish National Parks left us this legacy, but only because they cared enough to so. Let's not take it for granted. ***This*** is what it is all about.

Wither the Wild Wood?

This is a term we often misuse and most of our ancient woods are certainly not '*wild*' in that sense. However, the '*Wild Wood*' of the *Wind in the Willows* fame in the book by Kenneth Grahame, is real enough. It was based on a wood near Fowey in Cornwall.

So that's the place to go if you want to discover the real Wild Wood. I seem to recall that it was the haunt of the bad Weasels, but then I know a few Weasels in other places too.

It was also famous for the residence of Mr Badger. I hope Mr Badger is watching out very carefully just in case someone decided to gas him because they think he spreads Bovine TB. Now that really would be a shame.

The power of Rosemary

According to Robert Hackett in 1607, this garden herb is good for your mind. It '*...... helpeth the brain, strengtheneth the memory, and is very medicinal for the head*'.

Beech Trees at Longshaw. © Ian Rotherham

Now comes autumn

So we've had the '*Indian Summer*' for about a week and now we're going headlong into autumn. For the wildlife watcher this isn't such as bad thing. In many ways August is a quiet month for many birds and other wildlife. Ducks for example have gone into their moult plumage called '*eclipse*' and for a while are flightless and vulnerable to predators. For others the serious business of breeding and raising young is done. So the singing and endless activity to defend their territory, find and keep a mate, and then raise a hungry brood, has passed; all is quiet, at least relatively. For many birds there follows the annual migration which may be within Britain or can be across whole continents. This is now in full swing and we can expect the first autumn and then winter visitors to start arriving with us soon.

Some of the birds moving around at this time are the birds of prey. One of our main groups of birds of prey is the falcons, which includes Kestrel, Peregrine, Merlin and Hobby. These are different from the closely-related hawks such as Sparrowhawk and Goshawk, though lots of people traditionally lump them altogether as '*hawks*', and let's face it many people mix up

Sparrowhawk and Kestrel. There's been good views of Hobby around the region recently, and I've had records from both Derbyshire just south of Chesterfield, and from moorlands west of Sheffield. Late summer and into the autumn is a good time to watch out for these summer visitors as they move through the region and the local birds prepare for the long flight to their winter grounds. The Hobby is a rather stunning bird, and a similar size to the more familiar Kestrel but with a shorter tail and long sickle-shaped wings. Their upper parts are dark slate blue with a brilliant white underside flecked with black, and also very distinctive white face patches and a noticeable strong black moustachial stripe. The Hobby is altogether a very striking bird and made more so by the orangey-red feathering around its legs and under-tail. The legs are bright yellow. It is also one of the success stories of recent years having increased its range considerably; for us making a welcome difference as it has changed from a rare summer and migration time visitor, to a regular breeding species. The favoured habitat is heathland and especially southern lowland heath; hence its comparative rarity with us, but they do well on the moorland fringe. A major part of their diet is large dragonflies which inhabit wet moors and heaths, and areas such as fenlands and marshes, and these are taken along with other large insects and also small birds. Hobbies usually nest in a tree and use the abandoned nest of another bird such as a Crow. At this time of year, if you're lucky, there's always a chance of a family group of two adults and perhaps 2-3 youngsters.

We still have a continuing problem of sickening persecution of birds of prey, and theft of both adults and eggs. The Peregrine Falcon, the big brother of the Hobby, has had particularly persistent problems with egg collectors and with illegal poisoning in the Peak District. Even in the early twenty-first century, these problems still go on. But it seems they have done well somewhere locally this year. One of my colleagues at Sheffield Hallam University, Dr John Rose, saw a family party of 3-4 Peregrines have a tangle with a Buzzard close to where he lives. The Peregrines were moving through the local Buzzard's breeding territory near to Matlock. The Buzzard clearly took a dim view. One of the characteristic features of the Peregrine's behaviour is when they drop near vertically onto prey. They will have drifted high in the air, perhaps on a rising thermal, to a great height, often hardly visible to the naked eye. Then, they close their wings totally and drop like a stone. At the end of the '*stoop*' they strike the unsuspecting prey, usually to deadly effect. However, Peregrines will quite happily '*stoop*' at rival birds of prey if they are too close or there is a territorial dispute going on and that is what happened here. This is more at the playful end of the range of stoops available but even so it is best to get out of the line of strike pretty quickly. This is what John's Buzzard did, and quite smartly.

Lots of birds are now moving around; some are passing through the region and others either leaving or arriving. It is not just those birds which we consider to be migrants. So for example, parent birds that remain territorial may be starting to push younger birds out of their patch to fend for themselves. This is always a wrench with reluctant youngster not keen on working for a living. You have probably seen seagulls with the poor harassed adult birds pursued relentlessly by a clearly over-fed youngster that simply won't give up; the young (but very plump) bird's non-stop plaintive mewing would suggest it was starving. At first the parent birds do eventually feed, usually warm regurgitated fish, so don't try this at home! But eventually, after days of persistent harassing, the parents finally give up and the youngster is now alone in the world. Of course this is where all the body-fat comes in, because thrown on its own initiative the baby bird is not desperately competent and is genuinely and literally peckish. Watching gulls feeding at St Ives in Cornwall this summer I noticed that the older birds always but always get the prime scraps and other titbits around the harbour. In the mêlée of squabbling birds gathered around a half-eaten pasty, it is the older, experienced adult bird that swoops down and takes the prize. I don't like to anthropomorphise too much, but this does sound like humans!

Herring Gull. © Ian Rotherham

This is also the time of year for the fungi, the often hidden part of our ecology that are so important to making the world work. Fungi help to break down and recycle dead organic matter from both plants and animals. They also help '*power*' many plants by an association with plant roots called '*mycorrhizae*'. Amazing really, that when you look at most trees, all the heather plants on the moors, and even many plants in areas of grassland, they all possess these wonderful fungi in their roots. These are vital to their ability to take up nutrients. At this season, any trip to a local woodland or grassland area will provide chance to see many different types of fungi. An ancient wood such as Ecclesall woods in Sheffield will be especially worthwhile. But then so too will be any of our Birch Woods such as Blacka Moor above Dore Village. Here there are lots of different types but one very distinctive and obvious species is the Fly Agaric with its beautiful red cap speckled with white spots. This is one of the so-called '*magic mushrooms*', possessing chemicals with strongly hallucinogenic properties. It is the '*plant*' [more correctly a fungus] that the Vikings ate before going into battle to take away fear and to give them a feeling of superhuman strength. It is best not to try it at home as the effects are variable and can be a bit nasty. Check out any areas of old, unimproved grassland, perhaps on the moorland fringe or even in your local park, and there's a chance of some quite rare fungi called '*waxcaps*'. These are often bright orange, yellow or red and can be used by ecologists to asses the worth of areas of old meadows and pastures; so-called '*indicator*' species. If there's any animal dung about then look out for the '*ink caps*' which begin to self-digest from the edges of the cap. The largest one you're likely to see, often in groups on wider areas of roadside verge for example, is the '*Lawyer's Wig*' or '*Shaggy Ink Cap*'. This was used for a blue-black ink in times past, and if gathered early enough is good to eat. With fungi though, taking and eating is only for those who know what they are looking at. If in doubt, then don't do it.

JUST THINK...... if we each did one good thing for wildlife and nature every day then we would surely change the world.

Just a thought.......

The appropriately-named Waxcap fungi. © Ian Rotherham

I've had a couple of enquiries recently about birds apparently deserting local gardens. The concerned owners of the gardens want to know what is happening and why. '*Bird Lover*' of Sheffield 5 has had Blackbirds, two pairs of Thrushes, Blue Tits, and a pair of Wrens, but in recent weeks they have gone. There's even concern that a neighbour has a bird scaring device and this is driving the birds away. Apparently a contraption with a plastic pipe has appeared on the adjacent garage roof and is pointing at the garden. Could this be scaring the birds away? Well, the answer is probably not a plot by a disgruntled neighbour who doesn't like birds, but a more simple though less exciting explanation. I think all that is happening is that

the local breeding birds have fledged their young and moved out, as I described earlier. As well as this, the autumn is a time of plenty and often an over-abundance of fruits, seeds, nuts, and even insects. So basically the birds may simply be feeding elsewhere. The sensible thing is to perhaps decrease the amounts of food you are putting out, and maybe vary it with some Niger Seed (Thistle Seed) for the Goldfinches and Bullfinches, and Black Sunflower Seed for the others. You'll find that this will tempt them back pretty quickly. Also once the cold weather comes in, they'll be flocking to the garden again. As for the pipe over the garage pointing at your garden, I'm not sure what that is all about, but it will have no effect on the birds! The other enquiry was from Beryl Heathcote of Thorpe House Road in Norton Lees, Sheffield. She was also concerned about the loss of birds from the garden feeders, and the same answer applies. They have gone but they will come back. Beryl has a further worry. She has seen scatterings of feathers along some of the grass verges and in nearby Meersbrook Park, and these include yellow feathers, fluffy downy ones, and some tinged with blue. Are the big birds eating the little ones? Well, these sound a bit like the feathers from young Blue Tits and Great Tits, and yes it could be that the local Sparrowhawk is taking them. However, the good news is that it shouldn't have much effect on overall numbers and that isn't why there birds are not in the garden at present. Beryl remembers me from junior school days at Mundella or Norton County School, so it is especially nice to hear from her!

There are a few other interesting wildlife sightings at the moment, and it is a good time if the weather is reasonably warm, for late butterflies such as Red Admiral and Peacock, and for the big dragonflies too. One butterfly that is around is the Speckled Wood which is quite large and basically chocolate brown with cream mottling. Once very rare with us it has moved northwards and is now in gardens and woods all across the region. It was this species that Philip Helliwell contacted me about. He sent some pictures of:

'...*a butterfly which flew into my kitchen and after fluttering about for a while settled on the window and posed for some time. This butterfly has been around for a few days and I believe I saw it with another butterfly, possibly mating. It also flew into my raspberry patch, which is well populated by wild flowers i.e. weeds. I live close by you at Little Norton and have a good camera but unfortunately my abilities don't match it. However, I think the photos will be good enough for ID purposes. I have looked in my books but cannot match it. Due to the eyespots I think it's probably a Brown or maybe a Heath. It also looks a bit like a Marbled White so if all else fails I'll call it a Marbled Brown.'*

Humming Bird Hawk Moth. © **Ian Rotherham**

The '*Marbled Brown*' © **Philip Helliwell**

I think the idea of a '*Marbled Brown*' is rather nice and a great name. It looks like a Brown but is actually a White; so very confusing. The picture shows of the insect rather well. They are around now so watch out for them – the '*Speckled Wood*' or maybe the '*Marbled Brown*'; you never know this might just catch on. My other interesting sighting was a '*Humming Bird Hawk Moth*' in my garden last week when we had good weather. It is as it sounds a Hawk Moth and it looks and behaves like a miniature Humming Bird. This is definitely one to look out for and on a sunny day stands out as a rather orangey brown colour and flies like something from the old Thunderbirds series with a lot of hovering and vertical changes of direction. People really do mistake them for Humming Birds which of course you only get on the other side of the Atlantic. In gardens on the eastern coast of the USA, enthusiasts put out little syrup feeders for migrating Humming Birds to feed at. Not worthwhile here I'm afraid.

Peregrines overhead

Whatever the time of year, the great thing about wildlife is the unexpected. So just round the corner from BBC Radio Sheffield I had a very surprising wildlife sighting: a Peregrine Falcon. Stood outside Sheffield Hallam University quietly minding my own business on a street corner in pouring rain, I was waiting for a colleague to deliver a parcel. From out of town, he was struggling with Sheffield's one-way system. Even his SATNAV was of no avail. Well, having waited about twenty minutes, totally out of the blue and only a few feet over my head, a Peregrine Falcon flew lazily out of the swirling clouds and mist that were busy soaking me. It hung in the air on powerful broad wings; probably a female and maybe a youngster. It was hard to tell because although it was close, it was silhouetted against the sky; so not easy to be sure. Hanging on the breeze and flapping quite powerfully but slowly, it was unfazed by the hustle and bustle a little distance away on the street below. If you compare a Peregrine with our more common urban falcon the Kestrel, it really is a big, powerful and impressive bird. It seemed strange that such a magnificent bird and one so evocative of nature and wilderness, should be there just above the heads of so many people outside Sheffield Hallam University and BBC Radio Sheffield. You really expect such a bird out in the Peaks at Curbar or Stanage maybe, but not in the City Centre. I'm certain that nobody else saw it; we so rarely look upwards as we walk around city streets. There is a good reason for that, in that if we do, then there is always the problem of walking into lamp-posts, and I speak from personal experience! But now I was motionless and this wild bird drifted silently across the Sheffield's urban heartland. It seemed to be heading up towards the new tower blocks emerging by the Peace Gardens, and I wonder if it could perhaps be roosting there. This would make sense as their favoured site at Tinsley Towers has gone. What a magnificent experience though; I felt privileged.

Wouldn't it be great if some of our city centre developers were to put up a couple of Peregrine Falcon nesting platforms? When I was City Ecologist a local businessman offered to do this on the Tinsley Towers. This was back in the early 1990s and at the time a pair of Falcons had pioneered an urban colonisation in Derby. They were nesting on a cooling tower just like Tinsley at a city power station. However, the power company that owned Tinsley Towers at the time could not be persuaded to get involved. Imagine what interest would have been generated by a live video link to the Big Screen at Meadowhall. More recently in Derby City Centre the birds have nested on the Cathedral. Derbyshire Wildlife Trust organised a forty-two day bird-watch with telescopes and the website www.derby.gov.uk/peregrines had over 360,000 hits; if Derby can do it then why not Sheffield? Sheffield has often benefited from its glorious landscape setting and the rich tapestry of nature in and around the City. So this would be excellent PR for Sheffield and it could be on a new building or even an older one such as we have at both our universities. Do let me know if you can help!!

Now is the time to feed the birds

Anyway, that's your Saturday taken care of. But now, as the first frosts are setting in, is the time to get sorting those little jobs in the garden. With autumn passing swiftly by and winter on its way full tilt, if you have any spare time, then spend it tidying up and sorting the plants into the greenhouse or whatever. But then don't forget this is the time the local birds need a helping hand and it is worth stocking up the feeders now. Get the garden birds into the habit of visiting, so that when times get really hard they know where to go. Peanuts, black sunflower seeds, mixed seed and Niger seed are all good. The latter is also known as 'Thistle seed', and is great for Goldfinches and Bullfinches in particular. Fat balls are excellent food supplements for the

titmice and for woodpeckers too, but the Grey Squirrels will get through them pretty quickly as well. To be fair, none of these are cheap now and furthermore, the smaller the amount you buy then the relatively more expensive it becomes. In these times of financial constraints and the 'credit crunch' you might be tempted to forgo the bird feeding. However, please remember that they do still need to be fed, and think about the enjoyment, the sheer pleasure you gain from your feathered visitors. It ends up being pretty good value for money. Of course there are plenty of ways to help the birds through gardening with nature in mind. That is probably the cheapest way to enjoy wild visitors, but you need a bit of forward planning. I'll try to write a few helpful hints and ideas over the next month or so.

Autumn Beech. © Ian Rotherham

Finally, the seasons are changing and winter visitors are now streaming into the region. With flocks of Fieldfares and Redwings, the two northern thrushes, around Longshaw and Chatsworth last weekend, it is time to listen out for the Redwing's high-pitched but plaintive, *tseep tseep* call overhead in the late evening. Stand quietly outside most homes in the region at any time from 6.00 pm onwards and you will hear them. There are also numbers of Wood Pigeons migrating through and smaller birds too. Recently I've also noticed quite large flocks of crows, particularly Rooks, Jackdaws and Carrion Crows gathering in the mid to late afternoon in the Holmesfield and Dronfield area and heading westwards. These will be congregating at pre-roosts and then moving off to a favoured site late in the afternoon. I hate to be a harbinger of doom, but I always associate big flocks of crows or corvids with harsh weather. I'm not sure if this is really the case, but you've been warned and it might turn very cold this winter. Now that would make a change.

And so another year ends

On the high Peak District moors, it is perhaps winter that is the real season of this harsh landscape. Here when the soft snow has fallen and the blanket of white muffled every sounds save perhaps for the occasional sheep, this is our true wilderness.

Winter Ivy. © Ian Rotherham

In the long hard winters such as in the 1940s, the 1960s, and the late 1970s and early 1980s, it seems that the snow masks all boundaries. Wildlife driven by hunger and cold moved down into the lowlands and perhaps from say a bird's perspective, all the white areas were one. The urban and the rural merged and entwined. In the late 1970s, this was when Black-headed Gulls first came into feed and roost in some of our urban parks like Meersbrook. Common Partridge appeared well into urban housing areas such as Heeley, and in my parent's garden at Norton Lees we had a Reed Bunting visit the feeder for the first and last time. We also had a very distinctive one-legged Coal Tit but I'll tell that one somewhere else. I recall one especially hard and cold period when Paul Ardron and I were ranging far and wide over the moors around Ladybower, Rivelin and Bradfield we had the most remarkable experience. For several days the snow had re-frozen into a wind-swept ice sheet and the temperatures dropped lower and lower. Derwent and the moors were gripped by arctic-

alpine conditions and there seems no let up. Many sheep were lost, and even the Grouse were struggling. Then one day everything had gone. All the small birds, the Titmice and the Finches suddenly departed. Yet it wasn't just the upland birds that went. There were no birds in the garden either. It seemed like there was a sudden decision to move, presumably south and to warmer and easier conditions. It was either that, or the night-time temperature and the lack of food and water proved massively fatal. I'm still not sure. There were some spells of exceptionally cold weather in the mid-1980s, but never again such protracted periods with the icy grip of winter clutching the local wildlife so tenaciously. It was a harsh and hard time, but in its own way absolutely special and magical. To appreciate summer you need to experience winter; and the spring can be understood best, I think, by considering the colours and fragrance of autumn.

I hope you've enjoyed my book and I'd like to thank all those who have taken part in the *Wild Side* over the last few years, and in my other wildlife programmes and events over a much longer time. A lot of my published research over quite a few years now has involved records and sightings that you have sent in for the numerous surveys that we have run across the region. Please keep the phone-calls, letters and e-mails coming in. I do try to answer all of them but please remember that this isn't my day job!! All the records and observations help our understanding of nature and the natural world across South Yorkshire and the Peak District so do keep on sending them. There's an especially a big thanks to all those at the *Sheffield Star*. I'm particularly grateful to Paul License and Martin Smith, who have been so encouraging over the years and of course Rony and the rest of the team at *BBC Radio Sheffield*.

Kaye Meadows campaigners. © Ian Rotherham

A bit of background if you want to get involved with *On the Wild Side*

Dr Ian Rotherham, Director of the Tourism and Environmental Change Research Unit at Sheffield Hallam University, has teamed up with the Sheffield Star newspaper. He writes a regular Saturday column called '*On the Wild Side*', which covers anything and everything on the environment and local wildlife or conservation issues. He now also hosts a regular monthly phone-in, *A Walk on the Wild Side of Radio Sheffield*, with Rony Robinson on BBC Radio Sheffield. Ian welcomes your letters, comments, sightings and records *etc*. The aim is to help raise the profile of the region's environment and also to help promote the enthusiasms and work of local organisations. This is a chance to have your say and to support local groups and local wildlife. So please get involved and write in with information, records and sightings, queries, anecdotes, memories or grumbles and concerns about wildlife and the environment. These might be from today or memories of the past, serious issues or just interesting snippets.

Contact:
Dr Ian D. Rotherham,
On the Wild Side,
c/o The Editor,
The Star Newspaper,
York Street,
Sheffield, S1 1PU

Email: ianonthewildside@ukeconet.co.uk

Ian welcomes your letters, comments, sightings and records etc. but most of all your phone calls and emails to the programme. The aim is to help raise the profile of the region's environment and help promote the enthusiasms and work of local organisations. This is a chance to have your say and to support local groups and local wildlife, and importantly to have your say. Ian will do his best to answer your queries and questions, and to give you the latest up-to-date information on the environment, local, national and international. So get involved and phone, email or write in with information, records and sightings, queries, anecdotes, memories or grumbles and concerns about wildlife and the environment. These might be from today, or your memories of the past. It could be serious issues or just interesting snippets.

Contact:
Dr Ian D. Rotherham,
A Walk on the Wild Side of BBC Radio Sheffield,
BBC Radio Sheffield,
54 Shoreham Street,
Sheffield, S1 4RS

Phone: 0114 273 1177
Email: south.yorkshire@bbc.co.uk

See: http://www.bbc.co.uk/southyorkshire/ for Ian's web page '*A Walk on the Wild Side*' and up-dates!!

Also check Ian's website for information on events and on publications:
http://www.ukeconet.co.uk

THE SOUTH YORKSHIRE ECONET

Get involved – have your say!!!

About the author

Ian Rotherham is a Reader in Tourism and Environmental Change at Sheffield Hallam University. He is an ecologist and landscape historian by training but has also worked on tourism and economic impacts. With interests in forest and woodland landscapes he chairs international committees on forest history and the social and economic impacts of forests, and also sits on governmental advisory panels. Ian has published over two hundred academic papers, book chapters, and articles in magazines and national newspapers. He has appeared on numerous television programmes, both news and documentaries, in Britain, Europe, and the USA. When the South Yorkshire floods hit in 2007, he worked with the main BBC and ITV news programmes and with documentaries such as *Panorama* and the *World At One*. He has worked with local media for many years and in the early 1990s was the Radio Sheffield Ecologist at the old Westbourne Studio in Broomhill. He now teams up with Rony Robinson for a monthly *Walk on the Wild Side of BBC Radio Sheffield*, and writes a weekly column *On the Wild Side* for the Sheffield Star newspaper.

Brought up in Sheffield he attended Norton County (aka Mundella) School, and then King Edward VII Grammar School. He went to Lancaster University to read Ecology and then returned to complete a PhD at Sheffield University with a study of the invasive behaviour of the wild rhododendron. Passionate about nature and about conservation he set about gaining experience in both wildlife identification but also about site and conservation management. At the time there was very little teaching or training available on such things so it was a matter of hands-on volunteering with wildlife trusts and others. He was the Sorby Natural History Society's first volunteer Conservation Officer, and served on conservation committees for the Yorkshire Wildlife Trust, the Sheffield Bird Study Group, Sheffield City Council, and the Peak National Park. Ian was very involved in local adult education and training through the LEA, the WEA and Sheffield University, and through this helped set up several local wildlife groups, and was active in the early days of the Sheffield City Wildlife Group. In 1985, he was employed by Sheffield City Council to set up a new advisory service, the Sheffield City Ecology Unit. Despite this being the time of swingeing government cuts, the team grew though part-timers and volunteers to around twenty-five individuals and spawned the Sheffield Wildlife Action Partnership. This was critical in raising over £1 million for conservation in Sheffield and establishing for the first time a number of major Nature Reserves. Two particularly important sites which Ian pioneered were the reserves at Wharncliffe Crags and Heath, and at Woodhouse Washlands. With his colleague Geoff Cartwright, he was responsible for promoting the idea of a necklace of major sites around Sheffield, many of which are now managed by Sheffield Wildlife Trust and have received major financial grants for their care. Ironically, when sites such as Wyming Brook, Rivelin and Redmires were originally proposed they were strongly resisted by the committee of the Sheffield City Wildlife Group and senior officers in the then Recreation Department of the City Council, ...*because they were too much in the countryside… and we should only be promoting urban sites*'. This he considered a huge mistake since Sheffield people have grown up on the idea of access to the *WIDER* countryside and the Peak District; it is in their blood. But faced with intransigence, a partnership was set up and run successfully with the Yorkshire Wildlife Trust and Sheffield City Council to develop major nature reserves and environmental education programmes. The annual highlights were the *Wildlife Action Days* which each attracted around 10,000 visitors, and programme of around fifty annual walks and talks. A key to this success was work with the media, and especially *BBC Radio Sheffield* and the *Sheffield Star*. In 1991, Ian co-authored *The Sheffield Nature Conservation Strategy* which set down a vision for the future of the region's environment. He was also very active in the National Peat Campaign and the Sheffield Peat Campaign, and ran numerous Bog Day events!

It was also Ian's idea to form Friends' Groups for a number of sites, most notably and successfully for Ecclesall Woods in Sheffield. Here he battled for many years to get the Woods accepted into the South Yorkshire Forest area, a proposal strongly resisted by colleagues in the then Sheffield Countryside Management Service.

Finally, several years on when the Forest was reviewed, Eccesall Woods was accepted in, and so grant aid was available for essential work and the rest as they say 'is history'. A key philosophy of Ian's approach is local empowerment. He assumes that most, if not all people, are interested in, and care about, their environment. The key to action is then enthusing them about nature and helping to give them confidence to take action; in this way, we can change the world.

The author early 1990s, Grindleford Café famous for its notelets with hints to customers like 'Don't look at the chef – he doesn't like it' and 'Don't ask for mushrooms – we've never served them and we never will…. So don't ask'. But they served the biggest and best breakfast in the world after an early morning dawn chorus watch.